T0153891

The Chronicles of Nai Nai 奶奶

PRAISE FOR
The Chronicles of Nai Nai 奶奶
Beyond What Was Asked for or Imagined!

"This is an incredible story about a faith-filled woman and her faith-filled family, beautifully written by another faith-filled woman. But it's more than that, because the testimony of "Nai Nai" Chen is about God's love for the least of these, His faithfulness to His creation and to His own name, and His limitless power to make Himself known. And *that* is worth the read."

Dallas and Amanda Jenkins, Creators of the groundbreaking television show, *The Chosen*

"This exciting story reads like another chapter in the book of Acts! From China, to Taiwan, to America — divine guidance and provision are the norm. The result has been a top medical organization that Fortune Magazine says is *"changing the world."* When you read this book, the Chen's story will inspire you to step into the realm of *"all things are possible."*

Jason Peebles, President of WorldOutreach.org

"Cynthia and I have been blessed to know Mary Chen for the past 27 years and she is one of our most cherished friends. Her remarkable life story will leave you inspired and challenged. Mary is unique in her unceasing optimism and her straightforward, honest communication. Mary Chen is a truly authentic person who loves her Godly husband, treasures her gifted family and seeks to bless the world through hard work, generosity and service. She is a rare gift from God to those who love her, work with her and serve Jesus alongside her. I am thrilled that Mary's narrative has been written so people can experience her strong faith, sacrifice, hard work, compassion, and devotion to

Jesus, family and community. It is an honor for me to recommend her story to you and I know she will change your life for the better as she has mine!"

Rev. Larry Thompson, Founder and Executive Director of "Faith Foundry," and Former Senior Pastor at First Baptist Church of Fort Lauderdale

"It was my joy to be called "Pastor" by Mary and Jim Chen. In the library of people whose reputation is spotless and whose character is beyond reproach, this amazing couple are way up there on the top shelf. Few people have penetrated the culture to be "salt and light" as they continue to be Christ's own hand extended to multitudes in need of hope and help. This book is not just their story, it is the story of what God can do with you in the same way He did when two people yielded to Him.... Read it and reap!"

O.S. Hawkins, Ph.D. Author of the best-selling *Code Series* of devotionals including the *Joshua Code: 52 Scripture Verses Every Believer Should Know* and President and Chief Executive Officer of GuideStone Financial Resources of the Southern Baptist Convention

A True Story of Faith and Perseverance

THE
CHRONICLES
OF
NAI NAI

奶奶

Beyond What Was
Asked for or Imagined!

MARY SHAO MEI LEE CHEN
WITH KRISSIE SCHUSTER CILANO

NASHVILLE

NEW YORK • LONDON • MELBOURNE • VANCOUVER

The Chronicles of Nai Nai 奶奶

Beyond What Was Asked for or Imagined!

Published in New York, New York, by Morgan James Publishing. Morgan James is a trademark of Morgan James, LLC. www.MorganJamesPublishing.com

Proudly distributed by Ingram Publisher Services.

A **FREE** ebook edition is available for you or a friend with the purchase of this print book.

CLEARLY SIGN YOUR NAME ABOVE

Instructions to claim your free ebook edition:
1. Visit MorganJamesBOGO.com
2. Sign your name CLEARLY in the space above
3. Complete the form and submit a photo of this entire page
4. You or your friend can download the ebook to your preferred device

ISBN 9781631956539 paperback
ISBN 9781631956546 ebook
Library of Congress Control Number: 2021938880

Cover Design by:
Christopher Kirk
www.GFSstudio.com

Interior Design by:
Chris Treccani
www.3dogcreative.net

Morgan James is a proud partner of Habitat for Humanity Peninsula and Greater Williamsburg. Partners in building since 2006.

Get involved today! Visit MorganJamesPublishing.com/giving-back

DEDICATION

This book is dedicated to God and family.

God's mercy and grace made everything I am, everything I will ever be, possible. This book is one small example of His divine providence.

My parents, Minta and John Lee. From halfway around the world and across the decades, your strength and guidance reverberate throughout my being and influence my every move.

My husband, Dr. Jen-Ling "James" Chen. Your love, faith, and principles have been a constant beacon in my life. God makes all things possible, and your wisdom and guidance turn the possible into reality.

My children, Drs. Christopher and Gordon Chen. Two strong, independent, sensitive, God-loving men. As babies you stole my heart. As men you fill it with joy and pride.

My daughters-in-law, Stephanie Chen Esq. and Dr. Jessica Chen. Behind every successful woman are other successful women who share their faith and create a family's foundation. You have refortified our foundation and made it stronger.

To my grandchildren. There is no sweeter sound in the world than when you call me "Nai nai." Follow the teachings of the Lord and you will be blessed beyond what you can ask or imagine.

PREFACE

Two quarantined friends, one a missionary and the other the co-founder of a family-owned medical company in America, recently named by Fortune magazine as a top organization that is "changing the world," corroborate in putting the life story of the co-founder into writing. The true story was completed in short cell phone conversations

Mary Chen

over a period of twelve months almost to the day.

Beginning with evidence of the same belief in a living God in their family lines before both women were born, this is a fascinating study of how a living God made Himself known and gave evidence of His leading, providing, protecting, and giving purpose beyond what was asked for or imagined.

We thank God for the inspiration to put these events into a communicable work, and we are hoping that you, too, will find evidence of living hope in your own life as you read this account of how our living God loves us enough to save us...even from ourselves.

The medical company's co-founder, now in her 70s, is often called Nai nai 奶奶, the Mandarin word for "grandmother."

> *"Now faith is the substance of things hoped for, the evidence of things not seen."*
> **Hebrews 11:1 NIV**

INTRODUCTION

In a cloudy glass bowl on top of my mother's treadle sewing machine table next to me, a goldfish was mouthing something that I strained to understand but just couldn't. I might have listened to my mother then, but my appetite was gone. Everyone else had already left the table. On my plate lay a skid mark of mashed potatoes and none of the peas that I'd eaten one-by-one off a butter knife. A sorry-looking piece of cold, dry fish with skin on it was the point of dissension. I wasn't expecting my mother's uninhibited slap in the face. She didn't appreciate how I answered her, so she brushed behind me, yanked my hair, and broke the latest news to me, "*Eat* that! People in China are starving!" All of us kids knew that China was far away, and if we'd dig a hole deep enough, China's where we'd end up. That night I would've settled for a hole just deep enough to bury what was left on my plate.

Every war since the beginning of time had already been fought; still, that wasn't enough. At that particular time, China was embroiled in its own civil war. The country had taken a great leap forward in tandem with a great famine resulting in tens of millions of people dying from hard labor and starvation. Mom was right. People definitely were starving in China. Dad was right too, "You kids don't know how lucky you are to be living here in America!"

I was ten years old when Shao Mei Lee was eight. We grew up on opposite sides of the world, not knowing each other, each fascinated by a piano, yet making enough quality time to play cards, ride bikes, and compete at marbles in dirt circles with kids in our neighborhoods. We endured cruel nicknames while our early years slipped by without televisions, cellphones, or computers of any kind. An automatic dishwasher was a sibling, and Bluetooth was too far away for us to comprehend.

Both of us had a human influence who verified God's existence. Our superheroes lived in the Bible and our teachers at church taught us to pray. One of those teachers challenged my small class of girls to write in our Bibles, "Where will I be in ten years?" I'm not sure what I wrote then, but I'm *sure* my answer wasn't even close to what really happened!

Shao Mei Lee's family of nine was focused on surviving. She had a better life than most of the other Chinese people my mother was talking about, though. She went to good schools in Taiwan, an island off the coast of mainland China that had become a beacon of Asian democracy. Shao Mei Lee remembers running headlong into air-raid tunnels with her family while defense planes stormed overhead. She remembers an uninhibited slap in the face, too, when her eldest sister lambasted her for bringing home bad grades. Believing the slap was humiliating enough, Shao Mei's dad spared her from the usual punishment of being thrashed on her legs with a stick. We were both encouraged to get good grades, but neither one of us actually did. In the world's eyes, neither one of us looked like much.

Almost seventy years later, here we are: two friends, one a missionary returning to America and the other the co-founder of an American, family-owned medical company. During the pandemic of 2020, we spoke on cell phones each week for nearly a year from different cities to write Shao Mei Lee's story, a fascinating study of how a living God made Himself known and gave evidence of His leading, providing, protecting and giving purpose beyond what was asked for or imagined.

We thank God for the inspiration to put these events into a communicable work, and we are hoping that you too, will find evidence of living hope in your own life as you read this account of how our living God loves us enough to save us, even from ourselves.

To her grandchildren, Shao Mei Lee is "Nai nai" (奶奶), the Mandarin word for "grandmother." To her family, friends, and employees, she is Mary Chen, co-founder of ChenMed, named by Fortune magazine in 2020 as one of the top 53 organizations worldwide that is "changing the world!"

—Krissie Schuster Cilano

"Call to me, and I will answer you and show you great and unsearchable things you do not know."
Jeremiah 33:3 NIV

CONTENTS

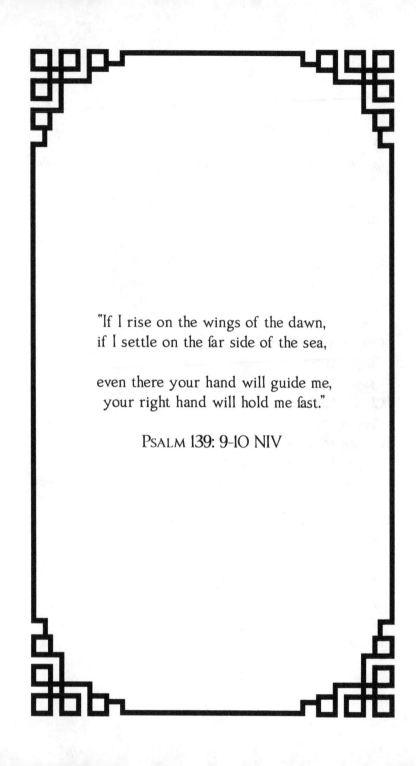

"If I rise on the wings of the dawn,
if I settle on the far side of the sea,

even there your hand will guide me,
your right hand will hold me fast."

PSALM 139: 9-10 NIV

CHAPTER 1

In 1944, the cause of a life-threatening disease commonly known now as "rat lungworm" was first identified in humans by researchers Nomura and Lim in Tainan, Taiwan. The parasite, first described in 1935 by researcher H.T. Chen, had been manifesting itself in a form of meningitis in people and had become epidemic in parts of SE Asia/Pacific. These parasites found in rats and rat dung were ingested by snails, slugs, and other mollusks, then transferred in slimy, little wakes onto vegetables. Vendors at busy markets were unaware that their goods were contaminated until the government put out a warning that eating improperly cooked snails or improperly washed vegetables was the probable cause of this frightening, deadly disease. At that time, there was no known effective treatment for *eosinophilic meningitis.*

The discovery came too late for Mr. Lee and his first wife, who had married much earlier in China. Mrs. Lee died of meningitis, leaving her husband with a baby boy who barely survived the affliction that left him brain damaged and severely limited physically. After seven years alone with his son, Mr. Lee re-married, this time to a woman named Minta, who would become Mary's mother.

Mary's oldest sister was seven years older than she. Next in line was another girl, four years older than Mary. Then, another girl, two years older than Mary, was born on a boat leaving China while the family was relocating to Taiwan. Born in Taiwan, Mary was the fourth Lee daughter. Four years after Mary was born, another girl was born to the Lee family, adding up to one, two, three, four, five girls and one half-brother, fourteen years older than Mary. Traditionally, Asian younger siblings were called by name or nickname, but older siblings were called *da'jia jia* (big sister) or *dah'guh* (big brother), a name that affectionately evolved to "Guh'guh" for the only male sibling in the Lee family.

A better-paying job with the Taiwan Power Company was reason enough for the family to move to the port city of Keelung in Taiwan before Mary was five years old. The Lee family lived in a big house with a big backyard that drew most of the neighborhood kids into playing Hide and Seek, Catch the Criminal, or marbles—much more fun than studying!

Ten years after Mary was born, a doctor delighted the family with his opinion that the Lee family should prepare to welcome another boy. Finally! And with a lot of excitement, the Lees anticipated his arrival. Mary's recollection of his debut is her father's *shushing* his five girls, "Be quiet...be quiet; Mommy is angry! New baby *not* a boy!"

Both parents worked in the same office. Mary's mom, Minta, typed; Dad worked as an accountant. Guh'guh spent time with them in the office. Family protocol ordered that older children were to take care of the younger siblings, so when Mary turned ten, she had two younger sisters to supervise, and she, herself, was supervised by three older sisters. Housekeeping frowned on backtalk, even though plenty of bickering went on among the girls. Everyone was expected to look out for everyone else. Loved and protected by the family, Guh'guh helped a lot with housekeeping but was exempt from key responsibilities. That was the Lee family.

In the house of six sisters, housekeeping and routines were mandated and delegated. Lunchboxes were made and taken to school every day for the school to collect. Then, all the food in the school kitchen was steamed at lunchtime.

"I *loved* food and couldn't wait 'til 12:00 noon, so I'd slip out of the classroom at 11:00 to find out what was in the kitchen," Mary remembers. "Then, I'd be first in line!"

"Did you ever get caught?"

"Not then, but I remember a time when I *did* get caught doing something I shouldn't have done!"

"What happened?"

"My father cleaned and collected our family's empty condiment bottles because he got cash or a discount trading them for new bottles of soy sauce, fish sauce, etc. One day, an old man balancing two baskets on a bamboo shoulder yoke came down our street. One of his baskets was full of used bottles and the other was full of candy. He asked me if we had any bottles to trade for candy, so I told him to wait right there for me. I dashed into the house, brought out all my father's clean, saved-up bottles, and made the trade. Then, I ate all the candy. Later, Dad was looking around, asking, 'What happened to all my bottles? Where are they!?' I got a big spanking for that!"

In 1960, the Lee family moved to Taipei, a modern, westernized city, very clean and advanced. One of the saddest days during that time was when Mary's oldest sister left the family in 1964 with a scholarship to graduate school in Kalamazoo, Michigan, USA. "When my oldest sister left for America, all of us cried," Mary recalls. "We couldn't believe that she was really leaving us. Papa cried and cried. I'll never forget how he sobbed."

To Taiwan, the Chinese brought Buddhism, Taoism, and Confucianism; the Dutch introduced Protestant Christianity and Spanish Roman Catholicism, and the Japanese brought

Shinto. There were animists, nature worshipers, and always the "lost," some seeking God, some wondering why on earth they were ever born.

Mary's family members were outliers who went to a small Taiwanese Christian church. Her grandmother and mother were solid Christians, along with her mother's sister, a woman named Hilda Chang, who lived to be 93 years old. She was an aunt that Mary never met. Mary never met her maternal or fraternal grandparents, either. At a young age, Mary's father was orphaned and raised by his older sister who had married well. Mary saw a photo of her, but she, too, was an aunt that Mary never met. As a child with a Christian upbringing, Mary memorized,

> [1] *"I lift up my eyes to the mountains – where does my help come from?*
>
> [2] *My help comes from the LORD, the Maker of heaven and earth."*
>
> **Psalm 121:1-2 NIV**

MARY'S FATHER'S OLDER SISTER WHO RAISED HIM.

CHAPTER 2

The five remaining Lee sisters inherited the responsibilities of their oldest sister after she went to America. Studying became even more important because the dream of being educated in America on a scholarship had become real. Mary's mother hired a tutor to prepare Mary's younger sister for her college entrance exam, and he wasn't just an ordinary tutor; he was a young man who had earned Taiwan's top score on the college entrance exam. His name was Jen-Ling.

The Lee family wasn't wealthy or privileged, but they knew the importance of family and education, especially for women. The Lee girls studied piano and eventually earned money tutoring piano lessons at home, giving them skills that would benefit them for life. Learning and teaching piano develops concentration, organization, discipline, patience, and, of course, time management by having to add lessons to an already busy routine. Math and reading skills improve with the counting and focus that is required in music. Coordination of brain, eyes, ears, fingers, and tapping feet all come into play with melodies, rhythms, tempos, and harmonious sounds. Learning to play a musical instrument often boosts self-confidence, reduces stress and anxiety, and can be great creative fun! Transferring a love of learning came naturally to a good teacher like Mary who was profoundly blessed with a strong foundation of good skills at a young age. "I loved my students," Mary remembers.

All earnings from tutoring were contributed to the family for whatever was needed, and the girls felt good about that. "I remember a time when I was listening to a quiet conversation my mother and father were having in the next room. They didn't know that I was around the corner listening, but I heard them talking about several pieces of jewelry they could sell to get money for our piano lessons. They sacrificed everything for us girls! We were so privileged to have parents who wanted a good life for us!"

While Mary dreamed of dancing and fashion and possibly having a career in those fields someday, the six Lee girls were growing up with the nickname "the six pigs," given to them by harsh neighbors. The Chinese zodiac has a sign of the pig usually meaning overall good fortune. People born under this sign are said to be sincere, giving, truthful, hard-working, and sociable with a large sense of humor, but this wasn't the reason the nickname stuck to the Lee girls. "Six pigs" was a cruel, degrading nickname for the Lee girls who would never have been called "pigs" if they had been boys! The Lees didn't pay any attention to the zodiac or to the nasty nicknames; they walked by faith as Christians, focused on the sign of the Cross and God's plan for their lives.

As the world turned into the 20th century, the generation of Mary's parents, the Soong sisters, who came from a wealthy, privileged family, inspired countless Asian schoolgirls by becoming among the first Chinese women to be college educated in America. Everyone knew about the success of the Soong sisters! Scholarships became available, and education for women became more of a priority in families who cared about the future of their children the way Mr. and Mrs. Lee cared about their own six daughters. With much studying and prayer before their decisions, Mary's two other older sisters went to America on scholarships. After four years at the Chinese Cultural College in Taipei, Mary, too, would receive a scholarship to Wittenberg University, a private liberal arts college in Springfield, Ohio, USA.

Wittenberg University is significant to Christians. In 1517, Martin Luther, a German priest and professor of theology, questioned the sale of indulgences, which in layman's terms were "tickets for forgiveness" sold by the Catholic Church. Fearlessly, Luther nailed a list of 95 questions and arguments for debate with the Catholic Church to the door of Wittenberg Castle Church in Germany, proposing that *salvation comes by faith and divine grace*, not from a faithful, unyielding obedience to a church or to a religion, person, or idol. This action sparked a worldwide uproar that resulted in the Protestant Reformation. Martin Luther was summoned to Rome and given 120 days to recant his accusations or be excommunicated from the Catholic Church. He did not recant, so he was excommunicated. For his own safety, Martin Luther lived isolated in a castle where he began translating the New Testament from Hebrew/Greek into German, the language of the people. In 1534, the Luther Bible was complete and ready to be printed. Martin Luther changed the way people reverenced God. Forgiveness and salvation were preached in the languages of the people, and worldwide hope came to life outside the Catholic Church.

Wittenberg University in Springfield, Ohio, prides itself, still today, on awarding scholarships to foreign and domestic students. In 1970, Mary would arrive at Ohio's Wittenberg University on a two-year scholarship to complete her master's degree, not in dance or fashion, but in choral direction.

While Mary was still studying in Taiwan, however, Jen-Ling, the tutor hired by Mary's mom, showed up every week to tutor Mary's younger sister. "I made Jen-Ling some noodle soup the first time I saw him," Mary remembers, "because he was *so skinny!* I felt sorry for him! I thought he'd do a better job tutoring my sister if his stomach wasn't empty! Besides that, he was tall and too good-looking to be so skinny!"

Jen-Ling watched Mary direct the choir at her church in Taipei before she went to America. "Then, one day Jen-Ling asked me if he could visit my school, the Chinese Cultural College, in Taipei," Mary remembers. "It was a nice day trip to my school, but I had to pay for the bus rides both ways for both of us because Jim's pockets were empty!"

Although they were becoming good friends, Jen-Ling wasn't a Christian. Mary told him right up front, *"I could never marry you because we would be 'unequally yoked.'"* The "yoke" didn't make sense to Jen-Ling. In fact, he didn't show up for the baptism that Mary arranged for him because he didn't understand baptism either!

"All the people were lined up to be baptized, and I said, 'Where's Jen-Ling?' He never showed up! Can you believe that? That told me something about his character, though; he wasn't going to be baptized just because *I said* he should be baptized," Mary recalls. "He wanted to know why. He was smart and looking for the truth!"

Jen-Ling joined a campus Bible study at his school, the acclaimed National Taiwan University, where he "met the Lord," as believers say, and experienced the truth of God's Word, the Bible. A thousand-mile journey began with that single step the day. Jen-Ling chose to make the love of God the center of his life. No turning back!

While Mary was at Wittenberg, Jen-Ling sent her a letter telling her that he was planning to start classes in St. Louis. He would be coming to the USA on a scholarship to earn a Ph.D. in biochemistry, and he wanted to see her again. In the handwritten letter, Jen-Ling told Mary that he had been baptized on Easter Sunday. "Now we're equally yoked!" Mary thought.

Months later, while at Wittenberg, Jen-Ling saw that Mary's visa was about to expire. "Like Esau in the Bible who sold his birthright for a bowl of stew, Jen-Ling was ready to trade his body and soul for many, many bowls of soup!" laughs Mary. Marriage seemed like the right idea to both of them, so the next day, in 1971, they were married "equally yoked" in Weaver Chapel in a small ceremony with one attendant. Mary and Jen-Ling "Jim" were both first-time dates who vowed to marry for life! They told their scattered families about their impulsive decision, brought on by Mary's expiring visa, and planned to have a celebration later when all their family members could be present.

If you visit the Wittenberg campus in Springfield, Ohio, you'll see the 212-foot steeple of Weaver Chapel as you approach the campus. For Mary and Jim's wedding in that Chapel that day, brilliant beams of color lit the stained glass inside the sanctuary. The newlyweds hadn't arranged for photos, but a professional photographer who was the boyfriend of a mutual friend was there taking wedding photos for them. "Look how God provided for us!" Mary says.

Everyone was invited to eat later at Mary's house. That would've been wonderful, too, except Mary said she made everything "too soon," and by the time the guests arrived at Mary's apartment, the food had soured, so there wasn't much to eat. But Mary's intentions were good, and she was a happy, radiant bride, and Jim was a happy, handsome groom, and it was their smiling wedding day with true friends who quickly forgot anything other than just being happy for the newlyweds.

The celebration with their families all together never happened the way it was first imagined, but who had the time or the expense for it? Their wedding was simply the best! Their commitment to honor God and to love and to honor each other in marriage for the rest of their lives was far more important than anything else. "Elaborate weddings are no guarantee that a marriage will last," says Mary.

God became number one in their marriage, and, at the same time, God became the center of their marriage. Prayer was foremost in every decision to be made as a couple and eventually as a family. God was alive and well. Their lives were placed in His capable hands to honor Him and to do things His way. He would protect them, provide for them, and give them peace and purpose.

[9]"Two are better than one, because they have a good return for their labor: [10]If either of them falls down, one can help the other up. But pity anyone who falls and has no one to help them up. [11]Also, if two lie down together, they will keep warm. But how can one keep warm alone? [12]Though one may be overpowered, two can defend themselves. A cord of three strands is not quickly broken."

Ecclesiastes 4:9-12 NIV

NEWLYWEDS JIM AND MARY CHEN.

Wedding photo, Mr. and Mrs. James Chen, August 1971.

Chapter 3

M r. and Mrs. Jen-Ling "James" Chen moved to Madison, Wisconsin, in 1973. Jim studied for his Ph.D. in biochemistry; Mary earned a teaching certificate. New friends at the University of Wisconsin in Madison had much in common with Mary and Jim, especially the Chinese Christians who met weekly for a Chinese Bible study.

A young, devoted Christian named Anan became a close friend of Mary. Both of their husbands were studying at Madison University; Mary and Anan were pregnant at the same time, and they both loved cooking for and eating with students who came to the Chinese Bible studies. Learning the Bible together gave them an understanding and hope that reached far beyond what the world had to offer. "It was a precious time of learning about God and His love," Mary remembers, "Everything we did was 'for the Lord.'"

Anan's first son was born in March 1976; two months later, Mary's first son, Chris, was born. Their babies played together, and those days became fond memories. Anan's husband, however, wanted to continue his studies in Boston, so that meant they'd be moving soon. Loving friends missed them even before they started packing for their trip! Anan's moving to Boston wasn't the worst news, however. The worst news came shortly after their move when Anan stopped answering the phone. No one was prepared to hear the unspeakably sad news that Anan had been diagnosed with advanced ovarian cancer.

In those days, being diagnosed with cancer, especially in its advanced stage, was a death sentence. That's how people saw it, and that's usually how it panned out. The disease took people of all ages in numerous insidious forms—lung cancer, thyroid cancer, leukemia, breast cancer, pancreatic cancer, cancer of the lymph nodes, tumors of all kinds, everywhere. Even pets died of cancer, and usually the death was a slow, painful process. Anan was the young wife of an aspiring scientist and the mother of a toddler. Still, cancer wasn't sparing anyone because of age or because of how important or loved the person was. Cancer plays no favorites.

Anan wasn't answering the phone, but when Mary persisted in calling, God allowed Mary's call to connect with her. Their deeply sincere, quiet conversation full of gratitude and reassuring promises to see each other again was clearly communicated. Then, Anan couldn't speak anymore. "Even my sisters said that Anan's death would be so hard on me," Mary says. "I don't know why God took her from us, but I didn't question Him. My faith is simple. The Lord gives and the Lord takes away."

Death stuns non-believers, especially sudden or unexpected death. We hear people say things like, "That can't be! I just saw him yesterday! I can't believe he's dead!" Without knowledge or belief in God, death can look like the deadest of dead ends. We learn about loss and how precious and fragile life is when our loved ones die. Some people become more cautious and begin paying more attention to their own health and habits in the wake of a friend's death. Some people go through a process of grieving, that is, coming to terms with their loss; others take years to accept the death of a loved one. Still, others never accept it. The death of someone can linger in our minds for a long time because of unsaid words of kindness or what could have been "…if only…" Pity those who are so afraid of dying that they never learn to live!

*"For God gave us a spirit not of fear but of power and
love and self-control."*
1 Timothy 1:7 NIV

Evidence of response to loss from death is everywhere. On a mountaintop village in Italy, old women covered completely in black clothing continue to mourn for the rest of their lives for their husbands who passed away years ago. They carry pictures and tell how they died. To them, there is nothing to be happy about ever again. In another town not far away, mourners remember covering their open mouths in disbelief as a young, anguished woman, resisting the force of pall bearers trying to hold her back, threw herself onto the lid of a casket being lowered into the ground and wept uncontrollably, *"Mamma…Mamma! Non posso vivere senza di te!"* (I can't live without you!) In a house on stilts in rural Thailand, friends will never forget the row of elderly women dressed in black seated beside a small box holding the body of a newborn at his funeral. He had been accidentally suffocated by his mom who rolled over on him in her sleep. The women in black swaying and crying, blaming the mother, saying God was punishing her because she renounced Buddhism to become a Christian are images that observers remember vividly for a long time.

Funeral rituals, some of which seem very odd to us, are ingrained in cultures throughout the world. Many are designed to send the spirit of the person off to a better world or back into this world to a new host. Some cultures celebrate the life of the person, some balance joy and grief led by a band of street musicians. A sect of Buddhists in Tibet and Mongolia believe that the soul lives on while the body becomes an empty, useless container, so they chop the body into pieces and leave it on a mountain top exposing it to elements and wild animals. Then, the soul is free to return to the earth to find a new body. In Ghana, the dead are buried in "fantasy coffins," large colorful containers representing something the person loved while he or she was alive, such as an airplane or an animal or a very large musical instrument or a favorite food. These ideas come from the imaginations of men, hoping for something better beyond this world. In a poem called "Thanatopsis," William Cullen Bryant wrote about death as an inevitable summons for each of us to join "the innumerable caravan," an apt description!

The Bible is clear that God's ways are higher than our own (Isaiah 55:8) and that it is appointed to each of us, whether good, bad, or indifferent, to die once (Hebrews 9:27). Real Christians, however, know the death-defying promise of God! To believers who share the hope of eternal life and of seeing one another again, Heaven becomes even sweeter knowing that loved ones are there waiting for them safely with Jesus, as promised. That's what Jesus taught us by His death and resurrection. Jesus appeared to believers after His crucifixion. He walked and talked and ate with believers by the Sea of Galilee. The Bible tells us that to be absent from the body is to be present with the Lord (2 Cor 5:8). We are told not to be afraid of dying, that "No eye has seen, no ear has heard, nor has the mind of man imagined, the things that God has prepared for those who love Him." 1 Corinthians 2:9 NLT

"God spared me the pain and sorrow of watching my best friend suffer before she died," Mary says, "and *I know for sure* that Anan and I will see each other again!"

> *"Precious in the sight of the LORD is the*
> *death of His faithful servants."*
> **Psalm 116:15 NIV**

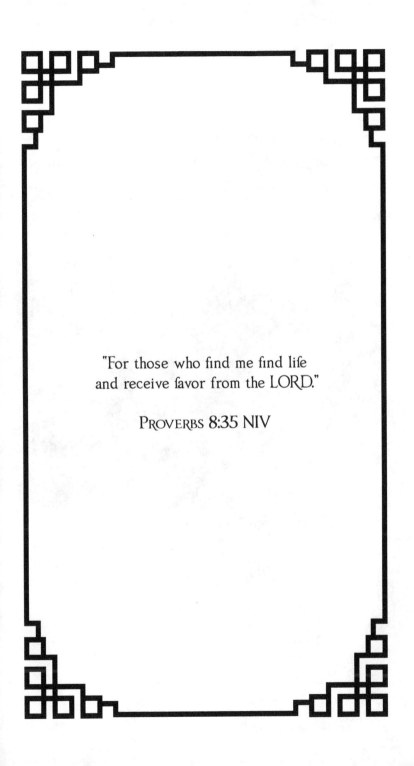

"For those who find me find life
and receive favor from the LORD."

PROVERBS 8:35 NIV

JIM AND MARY CHEN IN MADISON, WISCONSIN.

Chapter 4

Jim's older brother was coming from Taiwan on a visitor's visa soon, and when he arrived, a small, positive idea snapped all of them into motion. The idea sounded like a winner, and Jim's brother would be there to help. This was it: "Let's open a Chinese restaurant! We could call it 'The Great Wall!'"

While Jim spent most of his time studying, The Great Wall Chinese restaurant opened in Madison, Wisconsin. Mary worked hard at perfecting the restaurant, and soon The Great Wall was making enough money to pay babysitters for her son, Chris, and enough money after that to start up a second restaurant. With the Bible study on the back burner, and with enough cash flow, a third restaurant could open soon too. Mary made time to get her U.S. citizenship that year, while The Great Wall Chinese restaurants generated money.

Jim applied to the University of Miami for his M.D., but he needed a Ph.D. in biochemistry from the University of Wisconsin before he could begin the program. His helping at the restaurants was taking too much of his study time. Jim was privileged to be studying at one of America's top-ranking biochemical engineering institutes under the esteemed, internationally known Dr. Henry Lardy, and Jim should have graduated sooner than the six years it was taking him! Jim and Mary needed to "talk."

In that same year, 1978, Jim gave Mary a second, and final, warning: "You're so busy with the restaurants, Mary; you're turning away from God and our family! You promised to spend more time with our son and with Bible studies! You asked for a second chance, but you didn't change, so I'm going to pray that God takes the restaurants away!"

Mary's eyes narrowed, "Wait a minute, Jim! We're husband and wife! If I'm poor, you're poor too!"

"I know that, but I'd rather have a wife who loves God more than she loves making money!"

"But, Jim! If I make lots of money, I can donate it to..."

"God doesn't need your money, Mary. God wants your heart!"

In the wake of Jim's prayer to take the restaurants away, Mary tested the waters, "Lord, if you want me to close the restaurants, please give me a sign."

Jesus said that the sign will be the sign of Jonah: the man who was thrown overboard, encased in a whale's belly for three days, then spewed onto the land because he didn't do what God clearly asked him to do. The Book of Matthew records how Jesus answered the Pharisees and teachers of the law who asked him for a sign: "An evil and adulterous generation seeks for a sign, but no sign will be given to it except the sign of the prophet Jonah." Matthew 12:39 CSB

The sign of Jonah was a harbinger of Jesus' Resurrection after being in the grave for three days. Jesus said He overcame the world, and if we trust Him, He will lead us through this world into eternal life.

Mary was just wanting a sign about keeping open or closing a couple of small, seemingly successful Chinese restaurants and managing her and Jim's time better, right? That's all. So, what would that sign look like?

The matter was settled quickly. Within a week, a fire that started in another location in the mall spread to Mary's first restaurant, destroying it beyond repair; a week later, a severe snowstorm called a "nor'easter," blasted most of northeastern America. The sun melted big piles of snow and ice quickly, burying the second restaurant under severe floodwaters! The third restaurant never opened because there was no cash flow to sustain it. Bam. Bam. Bam. No one was inside the restaurants when the disasters occurred. No one was injured. God had spared everyone's life, so they were grateful for that! Words from the prophet Isaiah rang true:

> ²*"When you pass through the waters, I will be with you; and through the rivers, they will not overflow you. When you walk through the fire, you will not be scorched, nor will the flame burn you."*
> **Isaiah 43:2 NASB**

The restaurants were gone, the Chens were bankrupt, and Jim was getting close to finishing his Ph.D. in biochemistry. Mary had time now to pay more attention to her toddler, Chris.

In 1948, the year Mary was born, Carl Sandburg, an American poet, wrote this in his only novel, *Remembrance Rock*, "A baby is God's opinion that the world should go on." Mary probably didn't know about Carl Sandburg or what the poet thought was God's opinion, but one thing she knew for sure as the restaurants were being destroyed was she was pregnant with their second child.

"How can we afford another baby, Jim? We can't!"

"We can't refuse what God gives us, Mary."

"Okay, God," Mary conceded, "Now I want You to let me watch *this* baby grow!"

In a private conversation, Mary asked God, as she often did, "Did you forget your promise to me?" She was thinking that He had promised not to give her more than she could handle (1Corinthians 10:13), and things were starting to feel pretty heavy!

Seasoned Christians tell us that God sometimes allows things to pile up on us when we insist on doing things our own way, so that eventually when we can't "handle it" anymore, we call out to Him in a universal prayer, "God, help me!" to which He is always our first responder!

Jesus used this allegory, "I am the vine; you are the branches. If you remain in me and I in you, you will bear much fruit; apart from me you can do nothing." John 15:5 NIV Our Creator doesn't expect us to *make* the fruit; He asks us only to *bear* it! J. Hudson Taylor called this living "The Exchanged Life" (They Found the Secret by V. Raymond Edman.)

"This is God's universe, and He does things His way. You may have a better way, but you don't have a universe."
J. Vernon Magee

CHAPTER 5

On June 13, 1979, one day before the Chen family's second child was born, the University of Miami notified Jim that an immediate opening was available for him to start his M.D. program. Orientation was within the week, meaning Jim had to get to Miami faster than fast. With their second baby due any minute, Dr. Chen was ready with three girls' names for his new daughter. None of the names fit the newborn, though, because the newborn wasn't a girl! Gordon Lee Chen's middle name came from Mary's maiden name, and "Gordon" was the name of the doctor who delivered him.

"Your mother will be happy," Jim smiled. "Smart boy! He waited 'til his daddy got his Ph.D. before coming into the world!"

Jim flew to Miami, showing up late for orientation at the University of Miami. He was ushered into a hallway outside the registrar's office to be sorted out among the other Ph.D. graduates. There were only two lines, each plainly marked, "self-funded" and "in need of funds." One after the other, each Ph.D. recipient took a place in the "self-funded" line. There was no pushing or shoving in the lane where Jim stood, though, because he was the only Ph.D. recipient near the sign marked "in need of funds." He was flat broke financially. The registrar questioned him because he'd written "self-funded" on his application in 1978.

"Everything changed," Jim told her.

Still in Madison, Mary was loading their belongings into a red VW for someone to drive to Miami. The plan was that she would fly to Miami with Chris, Gordon, a few bags, and $700, all the money the family had. Theirs was a safe 4th of July landing at Miami International Airport. The three of them got off the plane with no stroller for Chris, no carrier for Gordon. Mary placed the swaddled, newborn Gordon on the floor of the Miami airport near the baggage claim and speaking directly into Chris's three-year-old face, instructed, "Watch Gordon! Don't let anybody hurt him or take him while I get our bags, okay?" From the luggage conveyor belt, Mary never took her eyes off Chris and Gordon. Family survival 101 was in session: We look after one another! This was the Chen family.

Jim showed up at the airport in a borrowed car and answered Mary's question about where they were going to stay, "We're going to look at a place right now..."

"But Jim...they'll want a deposit, and we only have $700 to our name! Did anyone from the church offer us a place for a few nights?"

In fact, a family from the church *had* offered them a place for a few nights. Mary urged Jim to call them, and the Chens settled in with very new friends for the first few nights. Then, a young couple with no children offered them a place for a whole month while the wife went to Taiwan to visit her family. Chris called the young man "Uncle," and the temporary dorm apartment for couples worked well, but not for long. The four-year courses at UM were jammed into two intense years. Jim had his head in the books. Everyone needed space.

Finding housing couldn't possibly be easy; the Chens were in the foreign land of Miami, Florida, not the Midwest anymore. Prices were much higher, and affordable housing was something needed by almost everyone you'd meet. The Mariel Boatlift was bringing 125,000 Cubans and 25,000 Haitians into Miami just then, so, finding an affordable place—what were the chances, really? Besides that, the crime rate was high. People warned them to be careful.

Mary picked up the phone the minute she saw the classified ad. Someone offering a free place to live needed a nanny! The woman who placed the ad was an American pediatric doctor whose husband was a professor at the University of Miami. She and her husband, who worked at the university, had an adopted son, two months older than Gordon, and they needed a nanny to clean their apartment and take care of their little boy while they worked. The accommodations were a furnished two-bedroom duplex. Even more, the duplex was in the vicinity of the medical school; Jim could walk to his classes!

The papers were signed, and the Chen family of four moved into the duplex without hesitating. That night, Dr. and Mrs. James Chen stared at a new ceiling from their furnished mattress.

"Jim! We are sleeping under a roof! THANK GOD!"

²"You know when I sit and when I rise; you perceive my thoughts from afar. ³You discern my going out and my lying down; you are familiar with all my ways. ⁴Before a word is on my tongue, you, LORD, know it completely."

Psalm 139:2-4 NIV

Chapter 6

2 "Consider it pure joy, my brothers and sisters, whenever you face trials of many kinds, 3 because you know that the testing of your faith produces perseverance. 4 Let perseverance finish its work so that you may be mature and complete, not lacking anything. 5 If any of you lacks wisdom, you should ask God, who gives generously to all without finding fault, and it will be given to you. 6 But when you ask, you must believe and not doubt, because the one who doubts is like a wave of the sea, blown and tossed by the wind. 7 That person should not expect to receive anything from the Lord. 8 Such a person is double- minded and unstable in all they do."

James 1:2-8 NIV

Moving from Madison to Miami firmed up Mary's faith, putting her at peace that God would continue to lead and provide for her family. Jim was enrolled in the University of Miami, they were in a house owned by a pediatric doctor, and they didn't have to pay rent. This pediatric doctor recognized that Gordon was showing signs of malnutrition and needed extra nourishment, so she took it upon her kind self to order special formula for Gordon until his health was restored. Mary applied for food stamps thinking, "I paid a lot of taxes when I owned my restaurants! Now it's time for the government to feed me and my family!"

Within walking distance of the University Medical School was a nursery and pre-school, taking in newborns to school-aged children. With the teaching certificate from Madison, Mary applied and was hired as a teacher of infants. Not only did she qualify for an income, but her two boys could attend the school at University of Miami gratis.

Eventually, the Chens had to give up the duplex, and Mary had to stop working as a nanny, but she found an affordable efficiency apartment nearby. Because she and Jim missed having the Bible studies, they started one again in their small efficiency. Mary cooked. Everyone sat on the floor because there wasn't a sofa, but the studies were rich, and no one objected to the cozy setting.

Not needing food stamps anymore, Mary went to the Food Stamp office to ask the clerk to take her name off the list.

"Are you sure?"

"Yes. I'm working now. You can give the stamps to someone else who needs them. We're okay now. Thank you."

The dumbfounded clerk gazed open-mouthed at Mary, "I've been working here 20 years, and no one has *ever* come in and asked to be taken off food stamps!"

Recognizing God's provision and protection was becoming a habit with Mary. God seemed to move Heaven and earth to allow Mary to watch Gordon grow as she had asked. Gordon was enrolled as a newborn at the University of Miami's "Debbie School," and every time Gordon was ready to move to the next grade, a teacher's position opened for Mary to be his teacher. "Can you believe that?" Mary says even now. "I got to watch my son Gordon grow through the newborn class and age five as his teacher! God really answered my prayer!"

Gordon was less than two years old, learning to tie his own shoes, when his cousin Jennifer came to visit. Her father, Mary's brother-in-law, was studying at the University of Miami too, one year behind Jim. He and his wife (Mary's sister) and toddler daughter, Jennifer, rented a house together with Mary, Jim, and their boys in Liberty City. Little Jennifer soon became Gordon's bodyguard at his own preschool. A little girl picking on Gordon enough to make him cry one day raised compassion for Gordon in little Jennifer's heart. She comforted her sweet cousin, "Don't cry, Gordie; I already slapped her for you!"

CHRIS, COUSIN JENNIFER, AND GORDON.

The year was 1980 when Liberty City took headline news nationwide for race riots and protests following the acquittal of four police officers in the death of Arthur McDuffie, a black, 33-year-old former U.S. Marine. Mr. McDuffie died of injuries sustained at the time of his arrest after running a red light at 80 m.p.h. on his motorcycle. It was brought out in the trial that the police ran over Mr. McDuffie's motorcycle to make it look like he'd lost control and been involved in a bad crash. The medical examiner, however, said that Mr. McDuffie's skull injuries weren't consistent with a motorcycle crash. The prosecutor said Mr. McDuffie's skull was cracked "like an egg" before he was transported to the hospital where he died.

Enraged shouts for justice ensued over the death of this black man at the hands of the acquitted police. People rioted in the streets, looted stores, and burned cars and businesses, thereby destroying Liberty City and adjoining Overtown. Eighteen people were killed, 350 injured, and 600 arrested. Liberty City smoldered for days in fires that burned most of it and neighboring Overtown to the ground.

Living in a rented house only a few blocks from one of the deadliest race riots to date in America, the Chens vaguely remember the noise of sirens, police cars, fire trucks, and civil unrest. They were focused on Jim's finishing his training to become a doctor, praying, reading the Bible, and raising their two boys. The Chens felt safe in the very unsafe Liberty City.

[11] "For He will order His angels
to protect you wherever you go."
Psalm 91:11 NIV

CHAPTER 7

While Jim completed his three-year intern/residence training at Jackson Memorial Hospital, the Chens rented an apartment across the street from Jackson in downtown Miami. Dr. Chen became a U.S. citizen that year. Chris and Gordon were both going to public school. Mary taught music in elementary grades at a public school, and Jim was about to begin his practice as a doctor. They sublet his first office farther north in Miami Gardens, Florida.

Jim's days were spent in his office. In the evenings, he visited patients in the hospital. Mary remembers waiting many, many times in their car outside the emergency entrance in the hospital parking lot with her two young sons while Jim checked on his patients at night. Even though Chris and Gordon slept in the car on most of those nights while waiting with their mom, they never complained about waiting for their dad while he did his rounds. They saw firsthand how their father and mother worked together day and night to provide for their family while taking care of others. Now and then, Gordon would "do the rounds" with Dr. Chen. He delighted in carrying his dad's medical bag with the stethoscope, blood pressure cuff, thermometers, flashlight, etc. He watched every move his dad made. Getting back into the car after doing the rounds one night, Gordon told his mother, "Yeah, it's very easy to be a doctor; all you have to do is smile!" Everyone loved Dr. Chen and his family, and his practice grew rapidly.

Mary drove Chris and Gordon to and from their school in the same red VW Super Beetle that brought their belongings from Wisconsin to Miami in 1979. By that time, the car was a certified rattletrap. Her sons told her years later that while they waited for her to pick them up on the curb at school, all the kids were laughing when they heard Mary come rattling down the road behind the wheel! More than one time the VW broke down, but, by God's grace, there was always someone who stopped to help them get going again. Mary would tell her boys, "See how good God is to us!" or if they were clunking along behind an open pickup truck with no tailgate carrying a load of unkempt kids hanging onto the sides of the truck bed and onto each other, Mary would tell her boys, "I'm glad we have our car! We can't complain!"

Often drivers honked their horns, pointed, and waved Mary off the road to let her know that smoke was billowing out of the engine in the back of the car. Worse than that was a time when she saw people running toward her in her smoking piece of junk with fire extinguishers. "I was always grateful for their help! Thank God for their help, and thank God for our car!"

....

The Bible has much to say about anger. "Don't be too quick to get angry because anger lives in the fool's heart." Ecclesiastes 7:9 CEB

Samuel Clemens, better known as Mark Twain, said it this way, "Kindness is the language which the deaf can hear and the blind can see."

Mary quickly starts another story, "One time Jim had something he had to do in Miami Beach, and I was supposed to wait in the VW for him. That day was sunny and hot. The car windows were open because there was no a/c, and it didn't take long for me to fall asleep. Jim is not usually one to lose his temper, but he was really angry when he got back to the car and saw a traffic ticket on the windshield, and I didn't know how it got there because I was asleep! "You have no sense of safety, Mary! And how could you sleep through getting a ticket?" But when we opened the ticket, it said, 'Warning: You can sleep in your car, but don't sleep in your car here.' Sometimes a good laugh is all that's needed to clear the air and make things right again, but we didn't laugh much about what happened right then."

"I had that red VW *Super* Beetle for ten years, and I was sad when I had to sell it," Mary reminisces. I didn't complain about my *Super* car because it made me feel *Super*! To me the glass was always half full; my mind was set on being positive, always counting the rescues not the breakdowns. I was so grateful to have that car!

Up until today, though, I didn't really know the difference between a VW Beetle and a VW *Super* Beetle. Turns out, the engines are the same in both cars, and there are only two inches more space in the trunk where the spare tire is kept on the Super Beetle! The tire in the Super Beetle lays flat because of those two extra inches! Can you believe that? We didn't have Google in those days!"

. . . .

At the beginning of his second year, Dr. Chen asked Mary to work in the office for him. With no medical office experience, but with plenty of understanding of how things should be done from her upbringing, life experience, and faith, Mary focused confidently on conducting the operational end of the business while Jim managed the clinical. Mary hired and trained employees, researched the rules and regulations, and made changes. She could have run the medical office management seminar that Jim asked her to attend because there was nothing new to her at the seminar. Mary was a natural with numbers and people, and she had come a long way from her first day on the job when the phone in the doctor's office rang. Mary laughs now, "I was so scared to pick it up! SO scared!"

But she *did* answer the phone, and once again, routines were mandated and delegated, and Chen Medical began to expand. Managers were hired to interview doctors and workers, and a lot of prayer went ahead of hiring new doctors and workers from every ethnic group. Life did not stop if mistakes were made; mistakes were seen as opportunities to learn. That is how they operated, and it wasn't long before Dr. Chen lovingly reminded his wife, "Mary, you're supposed to be working for me. When did that change?"

> [10] *"God has given gifts to each of you from his great variety of spiritual gifts. Manage them well so that God's generosity can flow through you."*
>
> **1 Peter 4:10 NLT**

CHAPTER 8

Initially, the Chens had hoped to open their first office closer to North Shore Hospital on 125th Street, but local physicians asked them to situate their clinic north of 167th Street. They ended up even farther north than that on 183rd Street, which was Miami Gardens Drive. At the time of opening their clinic, the Chens weren't aware that a community of older residents was situated directly across the street. By the second year in that small office on Miami Gardens Drive, Chen Medical was becoming well-known in the neighborhood. "Being pushed farther north was a huge blessing in disguise for us," says Mary. "Our clinic was in a convenient location for the people there, and they loved Dr. Chen!" The office grew fast.

The Chens had paid off their loans, established good credit, and were in a position to buy a house. Even better, a realtor showed Mary and Jim a house that was only a few minutes' walk from their clinic. Being able to manage with only one car would be a savings! Before long, they took a very big step financially and were living in their first purchased home in Sky Lakes, just off Miami Gardens Drive. This was a big house on a neighborhood lake in what seemed to be a very nice place. A wall-sized tapestry that read "GOD IS LOVE" was visible to everyone who entered their first home.

Both Dr. Chen and Mary were serious about quality education for their children beginning at an early age. Sons of the Chens were raised and held accountable for their actions with strong Christian family values. Dr. Chen's sons were on the right path to becoming good husbands, fathers, and community leaders.

Classes in the public school seemed large, and both Chris and Gordon had about six teachers each. "In July, I started putting small amounts of money aside to buy nice gifts for each one of their teachers at Christmastime," Mary remembers. "I wanted our sons to know how important it is to respect their teachers and to honor them with nice gifts. Christmas is a time for giving."

The Chens sought and found an exceptional private school in Fort Lauderdale where both sons could stay during the week and come home on weekends. The student/teacher ratio was 9:1, much better than what public schools could offer, and the school provided an excellent support system and a sense of community where students were respected and felt valued. Focus was on character, independence, and leadership. Students learned to "go the extra mile" and to adopt a mindset of doing something "better than the day before." Chris and Gordon were ready to learn to navigate in new, highly competitive, international channels by developing crucial 21st century skills.

On the horizon of the Chen brothers' future was a world that would not see everyday life the same as what they already knew. Remote controls, digital cameras, digital televisions, computers, internet, Bluetooth, and cell phones that could be carried worldwide in one's pocket were about to happen soon. There would be new medical procedures that no one had ever dreamed possible to eliminate cancers and other previously untreatable conditions. Robotic and laser surgery were still in their infancy. Such an exciting time to be a young student! The future looked bright for smart students, and both Chris and Gordon were on the starting line ready to run forward!

The school was expensive. Mary was the designated budget keeper in the family and the family business, so she looked for places where the extra money might surface—doing this instead of that, eating here instead of there, and making do with this instead of that.

Because they were Christians, tithing had to be factored into the budget. In fact, Christians are challenged in the book of Malachi to tithe—that is, to cheerfully give 10% of their earnings before taxes back to God. The following passage is the only place in the Bible where God says, "...put me to the test..."

"Bring the full tithe into the storehouse, that there may be food in my house. And thereby, put me to the test, says the Lord of hosts, and see if I will not open the windows of heaven for you and pour down for you a blessing until there is no more need."
Malachi 3:10 NIV

Mary calculated and recalculated the projected budget for the year. Jim had already put his priorities on paper. His first item was a 10% tithe before taxes.

"Jim, if we could cut back the tithe to 7% or 8%, we could come closer to affording to send Chris and Gordon to Pine Crest School." Jim listened. Mary went on, "Hmm – we might be able to stretch that to 8.5%, Jim." Mary bargained all the way up to 9.5% before Jim reminded her,

"Mary, the Bible says 10% before taxes, so we're tithing 10% before taxes."

"But, Jim—if we don't cut back the tithe, they can't go!"

"Then we won't send them to Pine Crest."

Mary wouldn't let go. "Maybe we can send Chris first?"

We'll deal with that when it comes, Mary. Gordon needs to be there too. Don't skimp on the tithe."

God keeps His promises, and accepting His tithing challenge can be life changing. Until you experience it yourself, though, believing it requires stepping out in faith, something we hesitate to do because we are unaware that our very limited worldly knowledge is what we use to evaluate our supernatural God. We live by trusting what we feel or see or think about what's right there in front of us. Stepping out in faith requires us to forget about what makes sense to us at the moment. We have to back off and get out of our own way before we can call on our Creator. Then, unless we take the time to watch Him work, we'll never see what He can do!

"Okay, we'll see what happens." Mary bit her lip as she wrote another check for their 10% tithe before taxes.

That year, Chris entered Pine Crest's boarding program in 10th grade. One year later, when Chris entered 11th grade, Gordon enrolled in 8th grade, and the brothers boarded together during the week. There were no discounts, no scholarships, no outside financial help. God kept His promise to provide.

"You know, math is my strong suit, but I never figured out how God stretched the money that year to send our boys to Pine Crest! God definitely did it; that had to be a miracle!" Mary admits. Not only that, but God continued to manage finances at Pine Crest for both sons every year until Gordon graduated five years later.

Dr. Chen and Mary employed less than a handful of people in their small office. It was at a time when the portable phone, known as "the brick," came into being. Until then, Dr. Chen wore only a pager (a "beeper") and ran to a pay phone or a phone in the office or his home to answer every signaled call.

Besides being bulky, the brick was costly. Only Dr. Chen had the expensive, cumbersome brick to ensure that no calls would be missed and that he could return every call quickly. Dr. Chen was a very busy, very loved doctor.

> [11] *"For I know the plans I have for you," declares the LORD, "plans to prosper you and not to harm you, plans to give you hope and a future."*
>
> **Jeremiah 29:11 NIV**

Chapter 9

Every sports enthusiast at the new school was happy to see two new guys like Chris and Gordon who, much like the invulnerable Jackie Chan, were wildly devoted to training, impressively strong, yet habitually encouraging to others. The brothers triumphantly believed, "You win or you learn!" The Chen brothers stayed at Pine Crest during the week, kept in touch with home via a payphone, and went home on weekends. They wrestled, skied, and played football, and they could empty a refrigerator with astonishing speed. Gordon was, in fact, the captain of the Pine Crest football team for two years.

Chris qualified three times to compete in state wrestling championships beginning with his first year ever wrestling! But it wasn't until Chris left high school for the University of Miami that Gordon made a big name for himself as a wrestler, too. He was only a high school junior when the Sun-Sentinel headlined Gordon, saying that Gordon's coaches tried sparring with him at practice, and they were "no match" for Gordon. In one coach's words,

"That (sparring with Gordon) probably wasn't the smartest thing I've ever done. He (Gordon) locked me up and stretched me out pretty good. He's just a harnessed rage. He's very aggressive and very physical."

The sparring coach complained that he thought he'd pulled a muscle in his sternum after sparring with Gordon! When the coach asked how they got so good at wrestling, the answer was simple, "We fight at home!"

Even after moving on to the University of Miami after high school, Chris took great interest in supporting Gordon's high school wrestling. Gordon was a phenomenal wrestler, winning 100 matches out of 111 during his four-year career with a 50-2 record (one loss each year) during his final two years. As a sophomore, Gordon placed fourth in the state and seemed unbeatable. During his senior year in high school, Gordon, with great determination, was on his way to St. Petersburg to accomplish the state wrestling championship as his one goal before graduation. He wanted to win for his brother Chris, who he says taught him everything he knew about wrestling and came so close to winning the state title himself.

Chris drove from Miami to Gordon's high school to spur Gordon on by practicing with him. The Chens hired a private trainer to teach Gordon to wrestle even better to avoid being hurt, and soon the whole family was on its way to watch Gordon win the Florida State Wrestling Championship. A national championship lay ahead of the state competition, and everyone was confident that Gordon would easily win both the state match *and* the national competition.

Gordon had won the admiration of his teachers, classmates, teammates, and coaches, who enthusiastically praised his character. His coach saw Gordon as "a born leader with strong convictions" and that "If Gordon says he's going to do it, I believe in him." The coach acknowledged that Gordon wanted to become an orthopedic surgeon in order to be affiliated with the sports world, a big part of Gordon's life, and that "Everyone who knows Gordon respects him and thinks the world of him."

"From the football field to the wrestling mat to the classroom, Gordon Chen has triumphed because of constant determination and drive," his high school described him to the newspaper. "His career has been about setting goals and achieving them." Another coach said, "When Gordon steps off the mat, he's the nicest, most polite kid you're ever going to meet!" (This quote came from the same coach who said Gordon was a "harnessed rage" on the mat.)

"The state championship, that's my goal," said Gordon, the already county and district champion. "I'm serious about accomplishing this goal, and I'm doing the work that will hopefully pay off in a couple of weeks."

> [9]*"A man's heart plans his way,*
> *But the LORD directs his steps."*
> **Proverbs 16:9 NKJV**

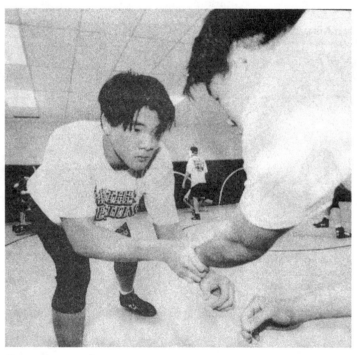

GORDON AND CHRIS PRACTICING NEW WRESTLING TECHNIQUES.

HIGH SCHOOLS

WRESTLING

Pine Crest's Chen pursues a final goa

By MICHAEL RUSSO
Special to the Sun-Sentinel

FORT LAUDERDALE — Pine Crest senior Gordon Chen's high school career has been about setting goals and working to achieve them.

From the football field to the wrestling mat to the classroom, Chen has triumphed because of constant determination and drive.

Chen has just one goal left to accomplish before he graduates — a wrestling state championship in St. Petersburg later this month.

"The state championship, that's my goal," the two-time county and district champion said. "I'm serious about accomplishing this goal and I'm doing the work that will hopefully pay off in a couple of weeks."

The ride to St. Petersburg begins for the 215-pound Chen on Saturday when he goes for his third straight district championship at the District 14-4A tournament at Northeast High School.

District tournaments begin today in Broward County with the top four wrestlers in each weight class advancing to next week's regionals. The top four finishers at regionals qualify for the state tournament.

Chen is 21-0 and can qualify for the state tournament unbeaten for the second straight year. He has won 100 of 111 matches during his four-year career and is 50-1 the last two years.

His only loss came in the state semifinals last year against the eventual Class 4A 189-pound champion. Chen strained ligaments in his knee in the first period but still finished. As a sophomore, Chen placed fourth in the state.

"I think that loss last year may have motivated him for this year," Pine Crest wrestling coach David Clayton said. "His goals before the year were to be an undefeated state champion and Broward County's Wrestler of the Year. If Gordon says he's going to do it, I be-

Staff photo/JIM VI

Pine Crest's Gordon Chen, top, works out with his brother, Chris.

lieve in him."

Clayton said Chen is a born leader, a respected student-athlete who everybody on the wrestling team looks up to.

"He's just a phenomenal individual," Clayton said. "I don't think anyone has come into contact with as good a person as Gordon. Everyone that knows him respects him and thinks the world of him."

Chen has a 4.2 grade point average and has earned a 1520 on his SAT. He says he's leaning toward attending the University of Miami or Brown University next year, hoping to eventually attend medical school.

He wants to be an orthopedic surgeon so he

can remain affiliated with the sports worl

"Sports is a big part of my life and I wan career that will keep sports close in my lif Chen said.

He says his inspiration has been his broth Chris, and his parents, James and Mary.

"Chris wrestled here and has taught me most everything I know," Chen said. "I wa to win the state title for myself, but mostly him, too. He came so close when he wrest here.

"My parents don't push me into sports general. They stress education. They're happy when I walk off the mat injury

NOBODY HAS A BETTER BROTHER

CHAPTER 10

With the Coach present, Mary looked straight into the faces of both Chris and Gordon. With her signature advisory tone, Mary began to lay bare the game plan as she saw it, "Promise me that if you win the state competition, you will *not* attend the national competition!"

The Coach heard what Mary said and had a look on his face that Chris and Gordon hadn't seen yet. The brothers nodded a sideways never, "No, no, Mom, we won't do that," but the wheels in their heads were probably telling them that they'd get past that later if they had to. The coach's eyes rolled into the back of his head. Everyone knew Gordon would win! Everyone wanted Gordon to win! Lots of screaming from the fans: *C'mon, Gordon! GOR-don! GOR-don!*

Gordon and his opponent in a neutral stance on the mat locked eyes, and as soon as the referee gave the signal, the shouting for Gordon sent the sound meter into the red zone. Gordon and his opponent, a returning 2x state champion, were trying hard to pin each other in an action-packed match with amazing takedowns, reversals, multiple lead changes, and surprise calls by the referees. In his corner, Chris was screaming so loud, nearing laryngitis. Mary and Jim would soon ride home with *GOR-don! GOR-don!* resounding in their heads.

Gordon once said accurately in an interview, "My parents don't push me into sports in general. They stress education. They're just happy when I walk off the mat injury-free."

Years later, Mary confessed to her sons that she prayed, "Lord, please let the other guy win because he needs to win more than Gordon does." She said this believing Gordon would be a better doctor than a professional wrestler, and everyone knows that Gordon is a champion in everything he sets his mind to already! So, while Mary was screeching, "Go, Gordie!" her prayer went right through the roof of the gymnasium, straight up to God with a trail of guilt hanging onto it like a heavy, wobbly kite tail.

Every athlete and sports fan in the 1960s watched a TV program called Wide World of Sports. If you followed or competed in any kind of sports, Wide World of Sports, like ESPN today, covered it. That's where the phrase "the thrill of victory and the agony of defeat" began, and that phrase became the famous opening of the sports program in 1970 after a ski-jumper from Yugoslavia, who during a European competition wiped out so badly that he flipped cameramen and fans upside down in his snowy wake. After he finally landed in a jumble, he begged the authorities to let him do the jump again, but they all gave him thumbs down on that idea, and Vinko was hauled away in an ambulance. The commentator sighed mournfully, "Oh, the thrill of victory and the agony of defeat!" ABC adopted that phrase to open, each episode of the number one sports program. Here's how it went:

> *"Spanning the globe to bring you the variety of sports, the thrill of victory, the agony of defeat, the human drama of athletic competition, this is ABC's Wide World of Sports!"*

So, totally by accident, the crash made Vinko Bogataj famous. He became known as the "agony man," and March 21, 2020 marked the 50th anniversary of his famous ski-jumping wipeout.

But Gordon *didn't* wipe out at the Florida state wrestling competition; Gordon wrestled hard and well. In fact, he was great! Suddenly, though, a rumble generated in the stands, and fans were protesting an unfair call! More noise, more dissension; soon, spectators were hollering and stomping their feet; the bleachers rattled like an oncoming train, and the noise of livid fans got louder and louder and even louder until the whistle blew.

The scene was reminiscent of a strike from "The Claw," the definitive hold of a famous Canadian-Polish wrestler in the '60s nicknamed Killer Kowalski who stood 6'7" and weighed in at 280 pounds. His classic hold, "The Claw," always brought a quick end to any match! Kowalski would clamp onto his opponent's face with his huge hand, thereby crushing his rivals into submission.

Stretch your imagination, if you can, to picture that while Gordon's fans were shouting their legitimate protests, Killer Kowalski's dreadful "Claw" seemed to resurrect itself into an eerie, room-sized intruder that clamped onto the faces of all Gordon's unsuspecting fans at once and tightened its grip! When the whistle blew and the final decision came through the loudspeaker, the phantom Claw released its evil clutch and slunk away, leaving Gordon's fans hurting and stupefied by the final call: the winning point for the Florida State Wrestling Championship went to Gordon's opponent! Who could believe it!?

Gordon could have won easily, even beyond this competition, but the match was over, the lights in the gym were turned off, and the other guy was going home with the title. The agony was real to the Chen brothers that night. Gordon's older brother Chris had accepted wholeheartedly the Chinese cultural tradition of being responsible for his younger brother. The loss left

Chris speechless. In good times, Chris could take some credit; in bad times, he took responsibility for what occurred seriously. "You have only one brother," Mary taught them. "You won't always have your parents. Family is so very important."

Getting ready for this match took hours away from Chris's studies at the University of Miami. His grades suffered, but that didn't seem to matter much to Chris. At the end of the competition, the brothers sobbed and consoled each other for a very long time. Their sorrow consumed them to the point that they wouldn't remember going to the car to go home. Everyone else who knew their pain was crying too. "The weeping during that loss still haunts me and makes me feel guilty," Mary almost whispers, her voice cracking. "I can still see and hear them sobbing. All of us cried. My sons worked so hard to get that title, and I prayed for the other guy to win, knowing in my heart that Gordon had a bright future even without the title." All of Gordon's fans went home knowing that the final call was indisputably unfair. Gordon should have won! Everyone still believes that!

Years earlier after watching Chris, Mary's mother commented that Chris would become a strong leader in whatever he decided to do, and she hoped that his life would be spent leading on the side of good. Chris certainly was on the side of good; he did his best to lift Gordon out of his grip of sorrow. The thought that "nobody has a better brother" was mutual between Chris and Gordon. The Chen brothers were a stronger team for the good and even more compassionate and empathetic than before the match. Not only had they suffered the agony of defeat together firsthand, but together they would recover.

Gordon would put aside his passion and ability for wrestling and focus more on his other passion and ability: football.

From there, he would go to Brown University in Rhode Island, where he would become captain of the football team in his senior year and play as a defensive lineman in Ivy League games. There may be more to consider in the unfair call that gave Gordon's opponent the title to the state wrestling championship, though. The young man who won the title didn't live long after that competition. Maybe that's why God gave him and his family that thrill of victory?

The Chens were avid sports fans, all right. A great time for the Chen family was watching the Miami Dolphins play football. Once in a while they would go to Miami to see a game live. Mary didn't mention if the Dolphins won or lost that night, but Chris drove them home with Dr. Chen in the front passenger's seat, while Mary slept in the backseat all the way home. Gordon, in his dorm at school, would hear the details of that night soon.

Chris pulled into their parking space in Miami Gardens and got out of the car first to go unlock the door of the house. Normally, Jim and Mary would have gotten out of the car and followed Chris right into the house, but when Jim opened the car door, waking Mary up, two men were standing in the dark next to Jim. Right about then, Chris came back to the car to see what was taking them so long. He caught on quickly when he saw a gun in the stranger's hand. Chris had walked right smack into an armed robbery, and these guys were holding his dad at gunpoint! Overwhelmed and spontaneously wanting to protect his dad, Chris rushed toward the gunman, fell to his knees in front of the thief, and pleaded,

"Please, don't hurt my father! He's a doctor! You can have whatever you want from us, but please don't hurt my father!"

The thief wanted Dr. Chen's beeper, but the good doctor said he couldn't give him the beeper because his patients and the hospital wouldn't have any way to contact him if they needed him. Suddenly, by God's grace, in his model, calm, sincere voice, Jim spoke to the armed trespasser, "How about my watch?"

Dr. Chen carefully removed his gold watch that Mary bought for him and handed it to the intruder. Barely moving, Mary was still in the backseat. She could see that when Jim offered the watch, the thief smiled exposing his gold teeth. The thief was satisfied. He took the watch that matched his teeth, and he and his accomplice ran away. The time had come to look for a house in a gated community.

³"But the Lord is faithful, and he will strengthen you and protect you from the evil one."
2 Thessalonians 3:3 NIV

CHAPTER 11

The new house in the gated community was west of University Drive, a long way from Dr. Chen's office. There was a lot of new construction in that area with almost no traffic. Road and street signs hadn't been put into place yet.

Annapur Road in the '50s and '60s was State Road 817 running through Broward County, Florida. It was renamed University Drive on maps in 1971. Not long after that, homes and businesses were being built there, and what was once seen as really far out west was actually east of the center of all the so-called progress. Eventually, new highways and overpasses made the long trips faster.

What we know now as toll road I-75 connecting Fort Lauderdale and Naples, Florida, was transformed from a two-lane dirt road through the everglades with no fences or barriers to keep alligators off the road or cars from plunging into the canals on what was then called "Alligator Alley." There were no gas stations or convenience stores, but there were plenty of broken-down cars and evidence of accidents. Travelers could stop at the few Indian villages along the way that offered tourists snake and alligator shows for entertainment. At that time, with no cell phones or telephones along the way, driving on Alligator Alley or on the Tamiami Trail from Naples to Tampa was at your own risk! The new communities, fashioned with green lawns, ponds, trees, and new roads and highways brought a new face to the swampy everglades.

While Chris was studying at the University of Miami School of Medicine Honors program, Mary and Jim were getting to know other Christians through Bible studies at their new home in the gated community. There was plenty of room in the new house for their sons to spend time with their friends who often stayed on weekends. The change was good for everyone. The Chens joined an active church in downtown Fort Lauderdale that supported missionaries in a poor community in Nicaragua and supported its mission effort in 1995-1996 by organizing medical mission trips with the missionaries there.

Not everyone is suited to be on a mission team. God is love, and a person on a mission team usually knows Him and the Bible pretty well. A mission-minded person knows that there is purpose in everything that is said and done and knows that wisdom comes from God, so usually that person isn't self-centered, but rather God-centered. A mission-minded person has most likely experienced God personally, and knows about His protection, provision, and promises. The mission is to know God better and to make Him known.

Almost always, everyone goes home from a mission trip changed, slightly or dramatically, especially if the person is one who sees God in action for the first time. The first moment alone with the living Savior can erase a lifetime of fear, guilt, and purposelessness, giving anyone who is willing to receive Him a new freedom that is greater than any other! A mission trip can be the most exciting adventure on the planet to a sincere believer because everything changes.

A foreign mission trip usually takes a first-time American team out of its comfort zone. Sometimes there's no drinkable water or the people hosting the team don't speak the same language or the hosts may have unusual customs, like eating with their hands or eating bugs or entrails of animals that Americans see as their pets. Before going, the team needs to be "prayed up" to be flexible and to remember who they are representing and what the real purpose of the mission trip is. The American high school students from the Chens' church formed their team and started training for their mission trip to Nicaragua.

Dr. Chen was the team's designated 911 medical response doctor who had to be equipped for any medical emergency along the way. The medical supplies that Dr. Chen brought for the team were used first, and any remaining supplies after the mission were donated to the Nejapa community.

Team members fell in love with the Nicaraguans, especially with the children. One team member said he thought he was on a mission to help a third-world country, but "they were the ones who changed my life through their selflessness and humility!" The team willingly left personal belongings, recreational equipment, and even their own shoes and clothing to their new friends in Nicaragua. Many went home calling it a trip of a lifetime. All of them had stories to share with friends and relatives back home, and many hoped to return to Nicaragua.

Half of Dr. Chen's staff went to Nicaragua with the team, so only a skeletal crew stayed back to run their office. Because the Chens were not physically present in Florida, the Chens would have to pay for the hospitalization of any of their patients while they were away. The Chens understood this and stepped out in faith praying that God would take care of their patients while they were gone. "*Not one* of our patients in Florida was hospitalized while we were on the mission trip! We looked over the records—that was the only month no one was hospitalized since Jim began his practice! God took really good care of our patients while we were in Nicaragua!"

"We were in a very poor area in Nejapa, Nicaragua. There were no flush toilets, and water was regulated for showers," says

Mary. "I remember being in a shower where there were a lot of huge moths, and I was scared, so I prayed that God would get me through the shower quick!" Mary didn't remember much water coming out of the faucet when she lathered-up with soap and shampoo, "…but I *do* remember howling out to Jim or whoever else could hear me that there wasn't any more water coming out of the pipe, and I was covered with soap!"

"Two things that will always stay with me from my trip to Nicaragua are: the kids who had *nothing* but were happy," says Mary without hesitating. "And the other is how the poor people respected and helped each other by giving everything they had to whoever needed it without arguing or complaining! They seemed to have genuine respect and love for friends and family. The kids didn't talk back to their parents or grandparents or teachers. Although I didn't speak their language, I am certain that they didn't criticize or gossip. It was a different world from what we were used to seeing back home."

Mary goes on, "We flew into the capital city and rode in buses to the village where the church, school, and place where the clinic would be. When I was getting off the bus, a woman among all the other women drew my attention. A very strong sensation overcame me and Jim, too, that we needed to speak with her. While this woman was saying hello to the kids and greeting the team with the other women, I indicated to her that we wanted to talk with her. With the help of a translator, my words were understood, and the woman's eyes welled up; she was crying and so were the other women who were with her. What I heard was that they didn't need or want money for themselves, but they needed money to keep the school open. Apparently, the government had ordered all public and private schools to close if they didn't raise enough money to pay the teachers a certain amount. The teachers had been praying that God would make a way to provide the money needed to keep the school open! Understand, this wasn't a school like the ones you and I went to; this was a school where children brought chairs from home so they would have something to sit on during the class, and the teachers gladly volunteered their hours to teach."

Mary gave the woman the money that was needed and went on to get settled and to help set up the tents and tables for the clinic. The team played soccer with the kids in their downtime and did what amounted to hard labor at other times—building onto the existing building, repairing what was already there, and painting walls inside and outside the school.

"To me," Mary says, "It reminds of the story of the Loaves and Fishes in the Bible. What we gave to the Nicaraguans seemed like so little, but God used what we gave to put the school in working order with additional classrooms. On our second trip there, we were deeply humbled to see a plaque in the classrooms with special thanks to the CHEN family."

[40]"And the King will answer and say to them, 'Assuredly, I say to you, inasmuch as you did it to one of the least of these My brethren, you did it to Me.'"
Matthew 25:40 NKJV

Chapter 12

Nicaragua, near the site of the Nejapa-Miraflores volcano, is short on cool breezes during the day. The American team was advised to stay hydrated in the extreme heat; nevertheless, some of the high school students passed out from heat exhaustion. One by one, Chris carried the volunteer missionaries to a cooler site to rehydrate and recover.

One of the American high school girls held out, though, withstanding the heat without complaining. She cared for the team members who couldn't help themselves, while the watchful eyes of the Chens were impressed by her selfless endurance. Stephanie, like Rebekah in the Bible, had the heart of a servant. When Abraham's servant was looking for a wife for Isaac, he asked Rebekah for a drink from the well (Genesis 24). Rebekah not only gave him a drink of water but offered to give water to his ten camels too! I don't know how many trips from the well to the camels Rebekah had to make to give water to all those hot, thirsty camels, but a camel can drink over twenty gallons of water if he's really thirsty! And there was Rebekah, most likely with a three-gallon jug on her shoulder, not complaining, just doing what she knew had to be done! That's how Stephanie appeared to Jim and Mary. So impressed was Mary that she remembered the girl's name, "Stephanie," and thought it might be a good idea to introduce Chris to her in a different setting once they got back from Nicaragua. Dr. Chen agreed.

Both Mary and Jim knew what American colleges and universities could be like, especially in bigger cities in the '90s. Sometimes there were so many worldly distractions (alcohol, drugs, sex, heavy peer pressure, to name a few), that not everyone made it out of college with a good chance of a happy, successful life ahead. Students dropped out; some overdosed, some ended up in jail or in rehab or in the morgue. Not everyone could "hack it." There were students who went to college with no plans other than to get away from a dysfunctional family or maybe to find a boyfriend or husband or both. U.S. college campuses provided an education, all right.

Graduate courses in medicine were tough, and to do well, successful students entered this level with a goal, plenty of persistence, and a good support team of friends and family who understood them and prayed for them. The Chens prayed for holy alliances for their sons, that is, friends on the same path who would encourage them the way their own Chinese Christian friends stood with them years before in Madison, Wisconsin.

Both Chris and Gordon were handsome, strong, smart, and on their way to becoming doctors, which mistakenly meant an easy future with lots of money to girls who fantasized that way about being married to one of the Chen brothers, and plenty of girls took a great interest in Chris when he enrolled at the University of Miami. When a summer college program opened up to study Spanish in Spain, Mary thought it would be a great opportunity for Chris to separate himself for a while, so he could learn Spanish, a good language to know both in Miami and in Nicaragua. "The time isn't right to be so serious about girls," Mary advised her sons. So, Chris experienced a summer abroad learning Spanish while the girls looked elsewhere for whatever they had in mind.

In 2001, Gordon went to Spain to learn Spanish, as well. Jim and Mary took the time to visit him in Madrid. "We had SO much fun," says Mary. "Gordon took us sightseeing all over

Madrid and to restaurants and to his school. We were asked not to speak any English when we were in public with him! At first, we thought our English wasn't really that great anyhow, and who would understand Mandarin (?), so we were quite comfortable with Gordon's wanting to lead the way and practice his Spanish. How funny that time still is to me when I look back! We clammed up, whispered to each other in English or Mandarin when we had to, and let Gordon do all the ordering and communicating with tour guides!"

Mothers and fathers who reverence God pray over their children, and no doubt, Mary and her beloved friend Anan prayed over their babies even before their sons were born in 1976. Throughout the lives of their children, believing moms pray that God will give their children direction through a beautiful world that is laced with salivating wolves. Sometimes parents throw their hands up and let their know-it-all children go their own way through the school of "hard knocks," but Christian parents try their utmost to redirect their children who would rather not listen to them.

We aren't promised a lovely world where everything goes our way; in fact, Jesus told us that his followers would be like "sheep among wolves," and that we would have enough trouble without looking for it, but "Take heart," Jesus told us because He overcame the world and would gladly lead us through it and even beyond.

> [6]"Train up a child in the way he should go; and when he is old, he will not depart from it."
> **Proverbs 22:6 KJV**

"For the Lord your God is living among you. He is a mighty savior. He will take delight in you with gladness. With his love, he will calm all your fears. He will rejoice over you with joyful songs."

Zephaniah 3:17 NLT

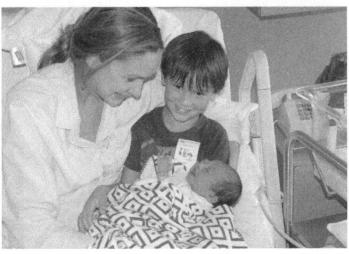

CHAPTER 13

To the untrained ear, a mother's persistence may sound like nagging, but if it sounds like nagging to you, know this: you may have an "untrained ear," and you should probably pray for understanding and wisdom, which God gives generously and without finding fault to those who ask. James 1:5

That's why Mary called Chris in his dorm to ask if he remembered Stephanie, the high school girl on the Nicaraguan mission trip who didn't pass out from the heat. "The tall, sweet girl?" And would he please consider calling her for a "date?"

"Are you kidding, Mom? Isn't she still in high school?"

Chris's roommates laughed like hyenas saying he'd be robbing the cradle, but Mary called every day with the same question, even though Chris's roommates could be heard in the background coaching, "Do it, Chris, just to make your mother happy, okay?"

Gordon was amused by it too. He couldn't imagine his big brother Chris on a date, I'd guess. Chris was "The Man" to Gordon, so cool, so athletic, so movie-star handsome, so successful, so independent, so... on and on with accolades. Gordon rolled on the floor laughing. But even that didn't stop Mary. She was sure Stephanie was the right one for Chris, so she kept calling, "Are you ready to date Stephanie yet?" before laying out a promise, "Just once, Chris, and if she's not the one for you, I won't call you about it anymore. I promise."

"Do it to keep your mother quiet," his roommates jabbed again until Chris caved, "Okay, okay, Mom! I'll call her, Mom! I'll CALL her!"

"Oh, no! No, no, no," Mary corrected him. "You can't just call her like that! I'll call her mother to get permission first!" Mary blindsided Chris and his roommates with a deadly verbal move that would have ended any wrestling match. Mary left all of them open handedly slapping the mat three times and tapping each other out for who knows how long before they realized they weren't opposing each other. "Uh," I imagine they said, "Maybe asking someone's mother for permission to date their daughter is just another 'cultural thing' from the old country?"

Stephanie's mom wanted to ask Stephanie's father, an attorney, how he felt about his daughter dating Chris. (Were Stephanie's parents from "the old country" too?) Finally, permission from Stephanie's parents was given, and Chris made the call in 1997. Chris was 19 years old; Stephanie had just barely turned 16. Everything changed.

Chris and Stephanie were married at an exuberant church ceremony with family and friends in Fort Lauderdale two years later in 1999. Gordon was Chris's proud best man. Mary's mother and father came from California to be honored at the wedding. "My mother loved Stephanie and told her, 'Be sure to have lots of kids!'" Mary says. All of Mary's sisters were there too. "We called the sisters 'Sister Number One,' 'Sister Two,' 'Sister Three,' (Mary was the 4th), 'Sister Five,' and 'Sister Six,'" Stephanie remembers, "because the Lee family still went by their Mandarin names or titles, and no one was certain of what those were in English!"

Soon Stephanie was on her way to college in Boston, and Chris was enrolled at Beth Israel Deaconess, a major Harvard University teaching hospital in Boston. The newlyweds, Christopher James Chen and Stephanie, were blessed with wishes and prayers galore to live happily ever after. They were "equally yoked."

*[21]"Whether you turn to the right or to the left,
your ears will hear a voice behind you, saying, '
This is the way, walk in it.'"*
Isaiah 30:21 NIV

Chapter 14

Chris's college roommate, Jason, was determined to become a doctor. He studied. Jason made such an impression on Chris at the University of Miami that both Chris and Gordon decided to get more serious about studying as well. Chris and Jason spent long hours together studying and eating. Sometimes Jason came home with Chris on weekends, mainly to "eat, eat, eat!" as Mary puts it. The Chens were delighted to have their sons and their sons' friends stay with them; all Mary had to do was make sure the refrigerator was full while they visited and to make sure there was enough food to go with them back to school!

In 2002, Nicaragua Medical Missions was founded, offering medical students from the University of Miami an alternative in lieu of other spring break activities. Gordon and the U.M. medical students' team were heading back to Nejapa. Once again, there were wide open smiles and happy greetings welcoming the young medical teams who were there to set up free health clinics and health fairs for the impoverished community. Pharmaceutical companies generously donated a quarter of a million dollars' worth of supplies for these Nicaraguan mission trips. Mary stayed behind to manage the offices; Jim accompanied Gordon and the team.

A University of Miami student named Jessica signed up for the mission trip, and Gordon's father couldn't help but notice the way Jessica moved carefully through the crowds with her selfless concern and compassion for anyone who needed assistance. Strength in her delicate frame was deceptive; she picked

71

up cases of water bottles as if they were empty and carried them to where they were needed and made sure everyone had enough to eat. Her smile put patients and co-workers quickly at ease. Gordon told his dad all about Jessica because they had become good friends.

As it happened, Jessica had worked her way through schools since junior high waiting on tables and doing what she could to take the financial burden off her parents. Jessica was studying internal medicine at the University of Miami. She was not only smart but pretty too, and not only that, but Jessica was the younger sister of Chris's best friend, Jason, who inspired both Chris and Gordon to study more seriously. Jason was like family already.

Mary and Jim knew when they met Jessica that she was the right one for Gordon. Jim couldn't wait to tell Mary about her after the mission trip. "You should marry her," Jim advised Gordon. "Dating too many girls makes it worse. When you find a girl like Jessica, stay with her!" Gordon didn't argue; he knew his dad was right.

When Gordon and Jessica announced their engagement, everyone was happy for them, but when they set their date for a wedding, everyone was even happier! Mary asked Jessica if she preferred a Chinese wedding where the groom's parents pay for the wedding or an American wedding where the bride's parents pay. No hesitation on that; the answer was "Chinese!"

Mary spoke privately with Jessica to let her know how happy she was that Jessica would marry Gordon and become an important part of their family. Their private conversation covered education, student loans, and what kind of wedding Jessica was hoping to have.

"Our family wants you and Gordon to have a 'fresh start' in your marriage," Mary told Jessica. By "fresh start," Mary meant debt-free. By God's grace, Mary was able to give Jessica a generous check for her wedding and told her that whatever was left after the wedding was hers to keep for herself. It's easy to believe, if you know Jessica, that she would rather pay off her school loans than have an elaborate wedding, but Mary took care of those school loans as well. What Mary meant by debt-free was exactly that! With much excitement, the wedding plans were set in motion for December 2003.

Everything was great. The business was growing; the Chens were even considering the possibility of opening a second office. Chris and Stephanie had been married for almost four years. Chris was working long days in a critical care unit in New York, and Stephanie was in law school there. Gordon and Jessica were walking-on-stars happy together!

On a late September morning in 2003, however, Jim woke up with an uncomfortable numbness in his face that seemed to be coming from a bad tooth. A dentist told Jim there wasn't any evidence of a bad tooth and advised him to get a CT scan, that day, if possible. Something was causing the numbness.

The CT scan revealed a mass embedded in Jim's sinus cavity. Was it benign? Malignant? So many questions! The sinus cavity is porous, like a sponge, and a mass that had wormed its way through the tiny tunnels of the sinus cavity would be extremely difficult, if not impossible, to remove! Even worse, the tumor *was* malignant, giving Jim "two or three months at most to live," the doctor told the family. Everything stopped and changed again.

The Chen family pulled together. "We're going to fight this!" Mary told some of her friends. Everyone came home. Chris's hospital supervisor understood completely because his family knew that delays are sometimes unavoidable. He told Chris that his critical care position at the hospital in New York would be waiting for him whenever he was able to return. Stephanie's professor was different. "You'd drop out of your classes because your father-in-law has cancer?" Stephanie knew she had to get back to Florida as quickly as possible with Chris. Her professor didn't know that Dr. Chen wasn't *just any* father-in-law.

Unstopped by seemingly endless frustration, Chris called every specialist he could find. Mary called friends who knew how to pray. Some were local, others resided in foreign countries; soon believers around the world were on their knees for the Chen family.

Prayer requests like this one inspire all kinds of prayers. Some are strong, forceful prayers commanding the tumor itself to leave in Jesus' name; others are prayers that beg God to do what they themselves see as what's best. No one knew for sure what the doctors were saying about the kinds of cancer cells or about a surgery that might require extensive, disfiguring facial cuts, or what Jim's chances of survival really were at that point. Often the Holy Spirit intercedes for speechless believers who are praying wholeheartedly for divine help in such emotional and complicated situations. Romans 8:26-27 tells us about that.

Eight time zones away in the middle of the night, a missionary heard Mary's prayer request. After kneeling at bedside and praying, the missionary who rarely dreams went back to bed and experienced this dream: "I was walking in a Halloween-like atmosphere, very dark and disturbingly noisy. Seeing a grim, rundown structure like an outhouse in front of me, I could hear crunching under my feet as I walked reluctantly toward the outhouse to open a door that I didn't want to open. When the door creaked open, the outhouse turned into a massive heap of dead birds soaked in what looked like oil from an oil spill in the ocean, very thick, black oil—right there in front of me! I covered my mouth and gasped, and I thought I could hear my heart breaking into pieces. My voice murmured, 'Dr. Chen loves birds. Does this mean he's not going to survive?' I waited. Suddenly, a single, clean white bird flew straight up from the center of the heap, and the heap churned and turned itself inside out to become a vibrant flock of clean, white doves soaring into a bright blue sky! Bare branches on spooky trees morphed into waving branches loaded with pink flowers like the ones at a cherry blossom festival. 'Is Dr. Chen on his way to Heaven now?' The answer was soft, sweet, and clear – a comforting voice that I knew, 'Dr. Chen will live to see many grandchildren!'"

To some, dreams are wishful thinking; to others, depending on what a person eats the night before or medications or the stress from life, dreams can be shockingly real, sometimes prophetic, sometimes seemingly ridiculous, such as the one in the Bible where Gideon overhears someone telling a dream about a loaf of barley bread tumbling into the camp, striking his tent "with such force that the tent overturned and collapsed." Judges 7:13 NLT Or, how about the dreams of Joseph in the Bible when he was a teenager?

Joseph dreamed that eleven sheaves of wheat bowed down to one that remained standing, and in another dream, the sun and moon and eleven stars bowed down to him, too. These dreams didn't go over well with his eleven brothers who were already fed up with Joseph being their father's favorite. They understood the dream to mean that the family would be bowing down to Joseph in the future!

Joseph's life reflects countless ups and downs from which God rescued him. He was thrown into a well by his brothers and left for dead, then, on a second thought from one of his guilt-ridden brothers, Joseph was hauled out of the well and sold to some traveling merchants as a slave. From there, the merchants took him to Egypt.

In Egypt, the Pharoah's official named Potiphar found favor with Joseph and put him in charge of his entire household. Potiphar's wife wrongly accused Joseph of rape, so into prison innocent Joseph went. More rollercoasting.

Joseph then interprets two dreams that happened on the same night from two different men, a baker and a cupbearer who somehow offended the Pharoah and wound up close enough to speak with Joseph in the same lockup. The dreams happened according to Joseph's interpretation, that is, within three days, the chief cupbearer was restored to his position, but the baker wasn't so fortunate. Three days from then marked the birthday of the Pharoah and also the day that the interpretation of the baker's dream occurred, "...the Pharoah will lift off your head and impale your body on a pole." Genesis 40:19 NIV

Joseph's story doesn't stop there; he asks the cupbearer to remember him, but the cupbearer forgets, so innocent Joseph stays in the dank prison for two more years. At that time, the Pharoah has a troubling dream about fat cows and skinny cows on the riverbanks of the Nile. The Pharoah went back to sleep and had another dream – this time about healthy grain and thin, scorched grain. Being the Pharoah, he sent for everyone anyone could think of to interpret his dreams. Aha, the cupbearer thought he remembered the young Hebrew Joseph, still in prison, so Joseph was cleaned up, shaved, and wearing clean clothes before he was brought before the Pharoah.

We have to love Joseph's answer to the Pharoah after he put Joseph on the spot to interpret his dreams: "I cannot do it, but God will give Pharoah the answer he desires" Genesis 41:16 NIV.

The dreams were the same, according to Joseph, and God was warning Pharoah what to do about an impending famine after seven years of prosperity. Fresh out of the dungeon, Joseph was made second-in-command under Pharoah! And later his brothers, who thought he was long-gone and out of their lives, showed up looking to buy grain in Egypt during the famine! They didn't recognize Joseph when they tried to make their purchase.

What a story! Eventually Joseph was reunited with his aged father who believed his favored son had been killed by a wild animal years before that, at least that's what Joseph's brothers told their dad after they sold him to the merchants. They smeared Joseph's colorful coat with blood, took the coat back to their father, and lied about Joseph's death.

Joseph's answer to his brothers were these immortal words, *"You meant evil against me, but God used it for good"* Genesis 50:20 NIV. Joseph was quick to forgive because that's what God asks us to do.

Another troubled ruler, King Nebuchadnezzar in the book of Daniel, required the interpreter of his dream under penalty of death not only to interpret his dream, but also tell what he saw in his dream! When the interpreters said it was impossible, King Nebuchadnezzar became so furious, that he ordered their executions. The next day Daniel was brought before the King after asking the King's officer a simple question, "Why did the King issue such a harsh decree?" Daniel 2:15 NIV. During the night, God revealed the dream *and* the interpretation to Daniel who walked closely with God all his life. Daniel's reputation became well-known for his accuracy in interpretating dreams.

The book of Daniel reveals prophecies about the world and its end, in case you might want to know. Daniel 2:25 NIV

And, it was Pontius Pilate's wife's who had a dream in Matthew 27:19. She cautioned her husband to have nothing to do with judging Jesus because in her dream she saw Jesus as "just," meaning innocent.

The Bible speaks of dreams and visions and sometimes prophetic interpretations of them. While the Bible tells us that too much sleep can bring about poverty, the Word is emphatic that our living God watches over us and never sleeps (Psalm 121: 3). He is deeply connected with those who love Him. Furthermore, He blesses His beloved with sleep (Psalm 127:2).

We are warned against false prophets, fortune-tellers, and those who are interested in telling us our future, especially for money. The Bible tells us there is only one mediator between mankind and God, the Lamb of God who paid for the sins of the world. That mediator is Jesus, the author and perfecter of our faith, as He is described in the Word.

> [21]*"My son, do not let wisdom and understanding out of your sight, preserve sound judgment and discretion;* [22]*they will be life for you, an ornament to grace your neck.* [23]*Then you will go on your way in safety, and your foot will not stumble.* [24]*When you lie down, you will not be afraid; when you lie down, your sleep will be sweet."*
> **Proverbs 3:21-24 NIV**

CHAPTER 15

Chris managed to secure an appointment within days for his father at M.D. Anderson Cancer Center in Houston, Texas, which was no small miracle. The Cancer Center is world-renowned in treating cancer like an unwanted intruder to the point of using an advertising campaign that draws a red line through the word Cancer! The waiting list is innumerable.

On Thursday night, Dr. Chen's uncertain future was weighing heavily on him to make a request of Gordon and Jessica. Not knowing what might lie ahead with his treatment or the outcome, Jim asked Mary to call Gordon to see if there was any way Gordon and Jessica would consider getting married before he had to go to the Cancer Center in only a few days. Mary made the call and spoke with Gordon about the December wedding being so far away. She told Gordon what and why Jim asked, and Gordon spoke right away with Jessica.

Not wanting their dad to miss their wedding, Jessica and Gordon quickly returned an emphatic yes, vowing to do whatever-it-takes to make it happen. Jessica told Mary not to worry about anything, saying that they would find the right clothes, and everything should be fine. Mary didn't worry. Christians have wonderful verses to stop their worrying before it starts! 1Peter 5:7 KJV tells us, "Humble yourselves therefore under the mighty hand of God, that he may exalt you in due time: *Casting all your care upon him; for he careth for you.*" So that's what the family did. The whole family prayerfully put their wedding with only 24-hours-notice into God's hands and didn't worry!

The family of God is a fellowship of believers like no other. They recognize the power of God's love over the ungodly love of power that the world offers. Pastor Larry Thompson said he didn't usually call members of the church to attend weddings; but, without being asked to do so, he got the word out instantly about the special circumstances involving Jim's prognosis and the change of plans for Gordon and Jessica's wedding. It was even unusual that such a large church didn't already have a main event going on the next day! An army of volunteers came together like an organized beehive to help make the event a wedding to be remembered!

Jessica's father let her know that a lot of boxes would arrive at the Chen residence later that day, and sure enough, Jessica's wedding gown and dresses for her bridesmaids were at the Chen residence on Friday. How unusual was it that the dresses were made, except for alterations, almost three months before the wedding date! Jessica met with her bridal party early on Saturday morning to make impromptu fittings for the gowns! Great bonding and fun!

Volunteers were decorating the sanctuary with beautiful flowers and candles, and someone was unrolling the traditional white cloth down the aisle for Jessica's entrance! Stephanie's mom miraculously found and delivered a wedding cake that would feed every guest at the reception in Fellowship Hall! The church was ready with music, and, as we like to say, the icing on the cake was a pianist and a Grammy-award winning vocalist who volunteered their talents! Everything was in place for a glorious wedding!

Chris had contacted a well-known pathologist to ask (beg) him to please get a hold of his father's tests for a second look because time was going by so fast that nothing seemed normal. On his own time, the pathologist sorted through boxes of hundreds of envelopes of specimens the morning of the wedding until he found Jim's tests. He rushed the specimens to a lab, examined them on slides through a microscope, and saw the impending results.

Meanwhile, Gordon and Jessica were at the church ready to be married in Fort Lauderdale that Saturday. The church was filling up with friends and relatives whose presence made the impromptu wedding one that would never be forgotten!

All of Mary's sisters and Jessica's family were there! Jessica's sister, who was out of the country, had been located; she got on the last plane to Miami arriving early Saturday morning – just in time to have her bridesmaid's dress fitted right before the wedding!

"Nothing was missing!" Mary talks about the wedding as if it happened yesterday. "We were overwhelmed by Gordon and Jessica's wedding that looked as if it had been planned for a year! When God is involved, nothing is missing!"

Mary admits that even though the time seemed to be moving too fast, it was really only the time on the clock that was speeding. It was if her eyes were out there seeing faces, moving lips, and people gesturing, but she was not really hearing totally what was being said in what can only be described as a loud vacuous silence. All the talk about how surgeons might have to radically cut Jim's face and what kind of cancer cells would do this or that hadn't taken first place in her thoughts at all. Mary was in suspension, more focused on what God could or would do than on hearing about gruesome details of what surgeons *might* do. After all, God was the expert on moving heaven and earth to answer prayers!

The groomsmen were lined up, Jessica's friends were adjusting her veil and taking lipstick smudges from kisses off Jessica's face, and even the music was playing when Chris got a call from the pathologist who couldn't wait to break the news to Chris about what he saw on the slides with the specimens that he examined that morning.

"Chris, your father's cancer is *not* what you think it is! It's a treatable lymphoma!"

"Thank God, thank God," Jim and Mary were heard saying right before going down the aisle to be seated.

Gordon and Jessica's wedding was impeccable, and as guests were walking to the reception in the church's Fellowship Hall, whispers had already reached the ears of excited well-wishers who spilled the great news of the misdiagnosis all over the room. Jim's misdiagnosis was hogtied and no longer such an ominous threat to his life! Even though Jim was facing treatment, hope seemed to be in the air. Usual smiles and tears seen at a wedding were topped with big hugs and shouts of joy!

Gordon and Jessica knew ahead of the wedding that their honeymoon would be on hold for a while. Chris, who realized for the first time that he may have to take all of his father's responsibilities as the head of ChenMed sooner than he ever imagined, was consumed with absorbing information from his dad who was more concerned about his patients and his family than he was about himself! Chris wanted to take his father to the hospital in Texas, but he had to step back to let Gordon have that honor. Chris couldn't possibly have learned all that his father and mother ever learned through experience, but he had to step up and trust God to help him. Gordon and his dad left the morning after the wedding to assess and begin treatment at the hospital in Texas.

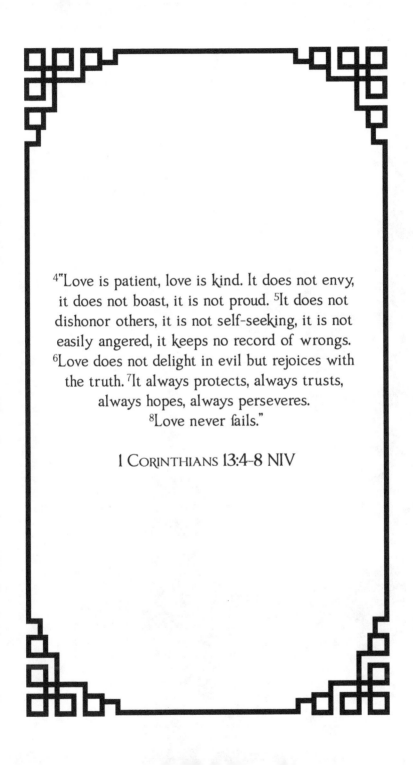

⁴"Love is patient, love is kind. It does not envy, it does not boast, it is not proud. ⁵It does not dishonor others, it is not self-seeking, it is not easily angered, it keeps no record of wrongs. ⁶Love does not delight in evil but rejoices with the truth. ⁷It always protects, always trusts, always hopes, always perseveres.
⁸Love never fails."

1 Corinthians 13:4-8 NIV

Chapter 16

The Chens coordinated trips to be with Jim for his treatments in hospitals both in Florida and Texas. The Chens had been thinking seriously about opening their second office, but these plans would have to be on hold until Jim finished his treatments in 2003-2004. Stephanie and Jessica rotated their visits during weekdays; Mary had to be in the office during the week, so she went to be with Jim on weekends. Chris and Gordon helped keep the offices going and took unscheduled turns being with their dad. Nurses and doctors took notice of the family's support. One doctor asked Mary, "What did you do to make your daughters-in-law so kind, so caring of their father-in-law? They bring goodies to the nurses and are always beside him for his chemo!"

Imagine having no family or support group behind you and being diagnosed with a deadly condition. Better yet, imagine a family who is dedicated wholeheartedly to being there for each other! That was the extended Chen family!

Dr. Chen, Sr., as a patient now, had plenty of downtime ahead during his treatment and recovery. The healthcare system made a shocking mistake with Jim's diagnosis! The family realized that six specialists had not consulted each other, even once, about Jim's treatment or care! But now was the time to be grateful, not only for his bright new hope of recovery, but also for the firsthand experience that allowed the Chens to scrutinize their own medical offices.

Jim trusted God to walk him through long hours of waiting in a sterile environment both at home and at the hospital during chemo sessions. Instead of sinking into self-pity or depression, Dr. Chen stayed keenly focused on what God was doing and how Chen Medical offices could improve in meeting the needs of their own patients. The Chens became a family of doctors brainstorming about becoming "the exception."

Jim studied the internet and learned everything he could about data and telemedicine. Finally, a stroke of genius came to him from what he learned online, and he was able to build Chen's own EMR (electronic medical records) system, an innovation that would thrust ChenMed way out in front of the norm for doctors' offices. Their offices would be easier to manage and even to duplicate! With Seniors being the select group of patients, Chen offices would soon be in a realm where all patients' records of diseases, conditions, diagnoses, and prescriptions would be available to doctors and specialists immediately via internet. This was HUGE.

The company became "paperless" with labs on the premises for quick results. Waiting for an appointment in six months with a specialist after being told by another doctor that you have two or three months to live wouldn't happen at ChenMed! Every patient's records and treatments would be coordinated among doctors and specialists. Every doctor would be in consultation with other doctors seeing the same patient. On-call doctors 24/7 and virtual visits would become an enormous blessing to patients after regular business hours. Patients would be afforded transportation to and from their appointments, if needed.

Not only because of their horrific experience with a misdiagnosis but because of the good that they saw in Jim's other healthcare workers who "went the second mile or beyond," the new ChenMed woke up to a greater commitment to serve. Routine visits were no longer "routine." Compassion plus the advantages of their Electronic Medical Record system dramatically improved the ChenMed way of serving patients. ChenMed employees understood that what was routine to them could be devastating and life-altering to a patient. Every ChenMed patient became a VIP!

Our ever-present, all-knowing God already knew the outcome of what began one morning when Dr. Chen thought he might have a bad tooth! If not for that, ChenMed might have become only a few more local, crowded doctors' offices in South Florida. Instead, the new ChenMed expanded exponentially after Dr. Chen's Electronic Medical Record (EMR) system drew attention from Medicare and all Medicare Advantage programs. Eventually Fortune magazine and even the White House would take notice of the way ChenMed strived to improve healthcare.

While a majority of doctors avoided Medicare patients, who were of the poorer, sicker, older population, ChenMed embraced them desiring to give them "concierge" treatment minus the membership fee (!) in their emerging centers. The Chens recommitted their efforts in serving Seniors, especially the underserved, the elderly, the poor, and the people who built this country. "They are the heroes," Mary says.

[28] "And we know that all things work together for good to them that love God, to them who are the called according to His purpose."

Romans 8:28 KJV

MARY CHEN IN HIGH SCHOOL.

CHAPTER 17

I Remember Mama was an American movie in 1948, the same year Mary was born. After that, it became a weekly American TV series, something every American watched for eight consecutive seasons from 1949 to 1957. Maxwell House Coffee sponsored the black-and-white program about a Norwegian-American family adjusting to life in America in the early 1900s in San Francisco. There was no remote control for the TV, so when the program ended, someone had to get up to go turn the knob on the TV to change the station. Often that person was asked/told to turn the volume up or down too, while he/she was there.

The Norwegian-American Mama, whose hair wrapped around her head in perfect light braids, managed the family, took care of the laundry, made three meals a day, shopped, balanced the budget, made the beds, cleaned the house, empathized with her four children who were all born in America, and comforted her tired husband who worked all day outside the home. With her sweet voice, she still had time to advise neighbors and friends over a cup of afternoon tea on personal matters. She was the gold standard of mothers in a loving family who shared happiness and heartbreak for eight consecutive seasons. Nobody we knew had a mom like that.

America had gone through a deep Depression in the 1930s. Money was still scarce in the '40s to lower middle class families. Another baby might have been God's opinion that the world should go on, but in some neighborhoods, another baby meant just another mouth to feed. American dads and moms were children during the Great Depression in America; they knew things could always be worse, so they were quick to let their children know almost every day how "lucky" they were to be living in America.

A loaf of bread in 1955 was 17 cents at our table, and Dad used to say, "You kids will live to see bread cost a dollar a loaf!" We laughed! McDonald's sold a double-patty hamburger for 15 cents and fries for another 10 cents then, but with those prices, our family couldn't afford to go there! Money was even scarcer in Mary's family.

"So, how about the cost of gasoline?" I asked Mary because at that time, a gallon of gasoline was 29 cents where I lived.

"Gasoline! What about gasoline?" Mary snaps. "We walked or took a bus! We never owned a car!"

"So, what did you get for your birthday?" I asked Mary, remembering my eighth birthday gift: some hand-me-down, latch-on, ball bearing roller skates with a key that tightened the metal skates onto my shoes.

Mary's recollection was as quick, "A bowl of chicken noodle soup with two eggs in it is what I remember. Eggs were expensive!"

Mary's mother had come from an upkept Christian heritage and was a strong Christian woman herself. She must've been keenly aware of what was happening politically and socially around her. When the neighbors called her six girls "pigs," Mrs. Lee ignored the hurtful name calling and told her girls to ignore it. The neighbors didn't know any better!

Mary's mom grew up in the era of the famous Soong Sisters. No doubt she was influenced by this family, whose story is here in a nutshell: The Chinese father of the Soong Sisters went as a teenager to work for his uncle in Boston. A Methodist tobacco magnate/philanthropist changed the course of Charles Jones

Soong's life by offering to pay for his education at Trinity College in America to become a Chinese missionary if he'd return to Shanghai to preach the Gospel. Charlie Soong took him up on it. He converted to Christianity, was baptized, mastered English and the Bible, and earned a degree in theology from Vanderbilt in 1885. He returned to Shanghai and met Sun Yat-sen at a Methodist church meeting in 1894. Both wanted change in war-torn China and both valued Christian western education.

Not making enough money as an evangelist, Charlie Soong began printing Bibles and later made a fortune in banking and printing. Eventually, Charlie Soong wanted western Christian educations for his children, three girls and three boys. He sent his three daughters to America, where missionaries met them and accompanied them to Wesleyan Female College in Macon, Georgia. Through great efforts of the Methodist Episcopal Church, Wesleyan Female College (originally chartered as Georgia Female College) became the first college in the world to offer women a college degree. All three of Charlie Soong's daughters' names appear in the records at Wesleyan Female College in Macon, GA, in 1908. Each of the Soong sisters was given an honorary Doctor of Laws degree in 1943. The legacy of these sisters is still evident around the world. They are well remembered at Wesleyan College.

All three of the Soong Sisters graduated from American Christian colleges, either Wesleyan or Wellesley College in Boston (Mei-ling, 1917). Mei-ling married well and eventually became a wealthy, generous donor to Wesleyan Female College. The oldest Soong sister, Ai-ling, married China's richest man and finance manager in the early 20th century Republic of China. She was the only sister to have children—four of them, and before she died of leukemia in 1973, she was given the honorable title of "Honorary President of the People's Republic of China." The middle sister, Ching-ling, "the Red Sister," married Sun Yat-sen, the first president of the Republic of China. In 1927, the youngest Soong sister, Mei-Ling, with her husband, Chiang Kai-shek, started the New Life Movement, a program designed to teach traditional Chinese values and western ideals.

Charlie Jones Soong accomplished much during his mere 55 years before he died of kidney disease in 1918. He valued education, and much like the Chens, he knew that his children needed to know what Christianity had to offer them and everyone else.

Eventually, the Soong Sisters were able to give generous gifts for scholarships to Wesleyan Female College. The Soong Ching-ling Foundation was instituted by the sister who married Sun Yat-sen. The Dupont Guerry Scholarship was a gift from Ai-ling Soong herself. The Mei-ling Soong Chiang Scholarship, established in 1944, continues today.

Wesleyan College eliminated the word Female from its name in 1917. In 1970, Wesleyan College became fully co-educational. In 1997, an anonymous gift of six million dollars was given to Wesleyan College for scholarships in honor of the Soong Sisters.

Wesleyan College is known for its "First for Women" ideology. The first woman to receive a Doctor of Medicine degree 1878, the first woman elected to the Tennessee legislature, and the first woman to argue a case before the Georgia Supreme Court were all Wesleyan College graduates. Other alumnae became architects, explorers, composers, authors, and scientists; still others moved into important political positions.

Scholarships from the Soong Sisters became available to girls internationally at Wesleyan College. In fact, Mary's mother's sister, Hilda Chang, the aunt Mary never met, graduated from Wesleyan College in Macon, Georgia, in 1948, the year that Mary was born.

THE GENEROSITY OF THE SOONG SISTERS BENEFITED WOMEN WORLDWIDE. MARY'S AUNT, HILDA CHANG, IS PICTURED HERE (ON THE FAR LEFT) WITH INTERNATIONAL COLLEAGUES AT GRADUATION FROM WESLEYAN COLLEGE IN MACON, GEORGIA, IN 1948, THE YEAR THAT MARY CHEN WAS BORN.

Now we can understand more clearly how the dream of Mary's mother became to educate her six daughters in America! She saw her daughters as being educated, valuable, influential women, not as "pigs." There is a lot of truth to the phrase, "I am strong because a strong Christian woman raised me."

According to Mary, her mother was "tough." There was no slacking on studying and no easy way of staying home from school. If Mary wanted to stay home from school, her mom didn't coddle her or feel her forehead to see if she had a fever. She told her to get dressed and go to school!

Mary's mom birthed and raised six girls and cared for one mentally and physically challenged stepson. She was self-taught at playing the piano and played only hymns. She worked as a typist in her husband's office where she typed on a manual type-writer *in Chinese*. For a moment, think about what a Chinese typewriter looked like in those days and how it worked! Some of the characters required using three or more keys!

Mrs. Minta Lee, Mary's mom, accomplished much in her 86 years. Remarkably, each one of her daughters was educated in a college or grade school in America. All of this happened in their family of nine who survived epidemics, illnesses, po-litical unrest, financial gains/losses, and ethnic criticisms and prejudices, without ever owning a house or car. Mrs. Lee taught her children to be compassionate toward those who had less in life, and although the Lee girls weren't smothered in material things, they had many things that could not be taken away from them, namely, a good education and faith in a living God. Mrs. Lee's legacy of being a driven Christian, lives on through her children, her children's children, and her great grandchildren, many of whom are Christians serving the underprivileged at ChenMed!

⁵"Trust in the LORD with all your heart and lean not on your own understanding; ⁶in all   your ways acknowledge Him, and He will make your paths straight."
Proverbs 3:5-6 NASB

Mary's parents.

CHAPTER 18

"My parents moved from Taiwan to the U.S. and lived in a house that my older sister bought them in California," says Mary. "One summer when our sons were very young, we rented an RV and took my parents to Yosemite National Park. I love to remember times like that."

The remainder of this chapter is in Mary's own words:

Hmmm... the last time I saw my dad was in California in the year 2000. He was at his home and very weak. Although he was pleased that all his daughters were doing well, he wanted desperately to see my older half-brother, his one and only son, our big brother, Guh'guh.

Years ago, Guh'guh walked with me to grocery stores in Taiwan. I can still see him carrying groceries with me back to our house and see him playing Hide 'n Seek or Catch the Criminals with my younger sisters and me. We were the criminals, of course, and Guh'guh was a policeman or a soldier. He was 14 years older than I was, an adult in age, but a child physically and mentally with a God-given immunity to cruel name-calling from people who didn't know Guh'guh the way we did. Guh'guh learned to read and write a little and tried to draw what he saw. He could dress himself and use the bathroom by himself, and he showed all of us how to appreciate life from a dramatically different perspective. Whatever happened, he was always happy! Our family loved and protected our vulnerable, sweet big brother Guh'guh.

When our family moved to the USA, we knew the transition for Guh'guh would be too difficult for him; he was 40 years old and had established routine work at the church where everyone knew him, spoke his language, and loved him. Moving to the USA would destroy his roots in Taiwan. We prayed as a family and with our pastor and his wife and our church family. A decision was made to allow Guh'guh to move into the church residence in Taiwan to continue his work there. He would not remember us enough to miss us, but we certainly missed him! Our family stayed in communication with our brother and the pastor and his family, and Daddy visited Guh'guh in Taiwan a few times over a span of 25 years. The return trips to the USA, however, became almost too physically and emotionally strenuous for Daddy as he aged.

When my father expressed a deep, deep longing to see Guh'guh again, I believe the Lord put it on my heart to inquire what it would take to have them meet again, this time in California. The long trip from Taiwan to California would require getting our brother a passport and hiring a responsible person who knew and loved him enough to accompany him on a very long, first class flight to America. Guh'guh had never been on an airplane! By God's grace, though, the plans eventually came together.

"Oh, he looks good!" my father told me when he first saw Guh'guh at the airport in Los Angeles. Because my father was so weak, I was holding onto him, walking him back to our car. In a very emotional moment, Daddy thanked me for bringing Guh'guh to see him again. "I have nothing to offer you, Shao Mei," he said. "I can only ask God to bless you," he said with all his heart. He could barely express his gratitude.

When I saw Daddy waving goodbye from his upstairs window, I didn't run upstairs to give him one last hug because I had to get back to my family and the offices in Florida. I waved back to him and walked away.

My father was a good father who loved us unconditionally. He treated each one of us like we were the only child in the family. He did his best to prepare us for what he knew about life. After his funeral, I missed him terribly. I thought about him in church one Sunday, and, almost as if everything was in slow motion, I became aware of being taken away from the service far enough that I couldn't hear what was being said by the pastor. At the front of the church, near a brilliant display of stained glass, I'm positive that I saw Daddy there telling me not to cry because he was okay where he was!

Today is October 20, 2020. My sister told me this week that Guh'guh stopped eating. Something isn't right; one thing Guh'guh and I always had in common is we both LOVE to eat! The 95-year-old pastor, who has been close to our brother for most his 85 years, told us that Guh'guh has stomach cancer, and hospice would be coming to help him get through his final days.

Today I am especially glad to know that because of what Jesus did for each of us, death is a transition to Heaven to be with Him. The pastor in Taiwan told us that our brother didn't suffer. After only a few days with hospice, Guh'guh went peacefully into the arms of Jesus. Guh'guh survived 85 years of living with profound retardation and brain damage from meningitis that he got when he was a baby!

This week, a devastating typhoon struck Taiwan, but the church was standing room only for Guh'guh's memorial service, we were told. Everyone knew him; everyone came. Christians who loved him dearly gathered to pray and to remember spending time with him. They sang hymns with words that because of Jesus they would see each other again in Heaven. Guh'guh projected happiness all his life. He didn't comprehend sorrow or anxiety. He didn't respond to anger or frustration. People in the church told my sister that Guh'guh didn't have a wrinkle on his face!

I understand more clearly now the depth of my father's desire to see his only son again after years of separation. Daddy knew that God had protected his son and provided a long, happy life for Guh'guh in Taiwan with genuine Christians whose children affectionately called him *"Shue'shue"* (uncle).

The longer I live, the more I love and miss them both. I think about my father waving to me from his window after we brought Guh'guh from the airport for his visit, and I remember not running up the steps for one last hug.

The next morning, after I flew back to Florida, I got the call. How could I have known then that Daddy would not live to see the next day!

> [4]*"Even to your old age and gray hairs I am he, I am he who will sustain you. I have made you and I will carry you; I will sustain you and I will rescue you."*
> **Isaiah 46:4 NIV**

Chapter 19

The jaw of the world dropped in the beginning of the year 2020, when COVID-19 started to make itself known. In late January and early February of 2020, a deadly viral pandemic was reported to be on a quick rise worldwide. The nature of COVID-19 was unknown early on. Scientists were guessing at treatments and prevention, like they were during the epidemic that struck SE Asia in the 1930s, the one that caused sickness from eating improperly cooked snails and improperly washed vegetables. Surprisingly, that parasitic nemesis is still making its rounds! In fact, a story re-surfaced on the internet about a 19-year-old Australian rugby player who was with his college buddies drinking wine at a poolside party watching a slug crawl by in 2010.

"Invincible" to his friends and to himself, he accepted a silly dare to eat that slug. Within a few days, he was thrown into a coma that lasted 420 days. He awoke as a severely paralyzed quadriplegic that required 24-hour care. He couldn't eat without a tube or move an inch without extreme effort. He died in November 2018. His family continues to tell his story, educating readers about "rat lungworm," the deadly disease that caused the severe affliction in Mary's brother, Guh'guh, at birth way back in 1935! Cases of rat lungworm are now well-established in over 30 countries worldwide, according to the World Health Organization!

If caught in time, rat lungworm can be treated with steroids and antiparasitic medicines now, but a total recovery doesn't happen often because the disease isn't easily identified in time for immediate treatment. The time between ingesting the parasite and getting sick is usually one to three weeks. Headaches, brain damage, fever, and other side effects can continue longer.

The statistics on COVID-19 deaths were too soon overwhelming in 2020. The most vulnerable were said to be elderly, especially those with existing underlying health problems.

ChenMed, whose patients were mostly elderly with multiple underlying health problems, was on guard warning everyone to stay safe, wash their hands, wear masks, and stay at home, if possible. These were all guidelines from the Center of Disease Control and World Health Organization. To be safe, Chris and Gordon ordered their parents to work from home, to not allow visitors, and to make grocery lists that would be delivered by family members.

Schools started to close. Students felt robbed of their high school and college graduations that were celebrated virtually online, if at all. There were no hugs, no kisses, simply no live, face-to-face pomp and circumstances of any kind. Restaurants, businesses, and churches were ordered closed. Flights were canceled, cruises too. Hotels and resorts were closed. Even beaches were closed!

Testing sites were set up, and anyone who tested positive was quarantined. Hospitals needed respirators, ventilators, and masks. Everyone was caught off guard! Thousands of people were dying, many of them were first responders, medical workers, and civil servants. Not every city could cope with the losses. In May, New York experienced so many deaths that refrigerated trucks were used to store the deceased, the media reported. Hospitals and nursing homes were closed to visitors. Drastic measures brought on an eeriness in the streets that few people had ever witnessed except in the movies. People were ordered to wear masks and to "social distance." Who could believe this was happening in America! But COVID-19 struck worldwide in 2020.

In July, Dr. Chris Chen was in great shape. In fact, he was thinking about signing up for a triathlon until one morning when he just didn't feel 100%. Maybe it was only a touch of the flu? But in less than a week, he was strapped to an ICU hospital bed, saturated in his own sweat, and unable to breathe in more oxygen than what he could suck through a straw. At age 44, Chris had contracted COVID-19, the pandemic virus believed to strike only the elderly who had underlying health issues. To Dr. Chris Chen and his family, things looked scary-blurry at best.

Fully masked, gowned nurses with foot coverings didn't stay with Chris in the ICU more than two minutes. Doctors tapped on the glass window and called Chris on his cell phone to let him know he was in "good hands." Chris hadn't felt a human touch since he left his house and was feeling progressively sicker. A touch from his four children and his wife would've done it, but hospitals remained closed. No one was allowed to visit Chris.

Who even *knew* what to do about this new virus that was causing worldwide panic and wiping out thousands of people!? Gordon took charge of Chris's responsibilities and contacted everyone he knew that might be able to advise or help his brother Chris. Gordon wasn't stopped by discouraging answers to his need for what was in extremely short supply. The Chens were buckling down, about to look for a glimmer of light in another, lengthy dark tunnel. "I was numb when I heard that our son Chris was struggling with COVID-19 in an ICU, and no one could visit him! We called everyone we knew to pray for him!"

says Mary. Gordon was trying to get plasma and one of the new drugs for Chris, but the drug was ridiculously expensive and scarce.

The Chens had to trust God to lead them in every decision and provide what they needed; they had to believe that God is who He says He is, despite a very nagging darkness that hung onto them like a short coat.

> [7] *"So that everyone he has made may know His work, He stops all people from their labor."*
> **Job 37:7 NIV**

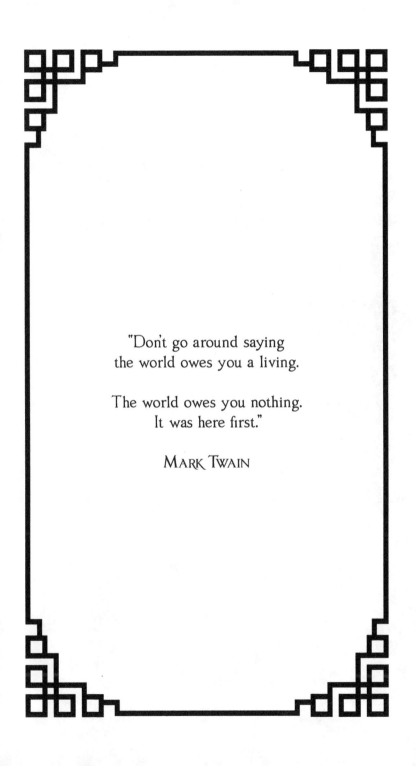

"Don't go around saying
the world owes you a living.

The world owes you nothing.
It was here first."

MARK TWAIN

CHAPTER 20

Finding our way in darkness wasn't meant to be easy for humans. Bats and other nocturnal creatures can do it easily and naturally, but without man-made inventions and equipment or divine intervention, humans physically cannot. We read and hear of miners who have survived being trapped underground for days in conditions so dark that they couldn't see their own hands. What thoughts kept them alive? True accounts of believers who have endured terrible and uncertain times often reveal that they remembered a Bible scripture or felt a presence or a whispered word that gave them hope.

Corrie ten Boom, a Nazi concentration camp survivor, relates going through deep darkness to being on an underground train through the Alps. "When a train goes through a tunnel and it gets dark, you don't throw away the ticket and jump off. You sit still and trust the engineer," she said in her definitive, thick Dutch accent, when she talked about her Savior, Jesus. Corrie and her family were solid Christians who took care of Jewish people who were escaping the Nazi death camps. She authored *The Hiding Place* and survived brutally dark days by remembering scriptures that she learned as a child. "You can never learn that Christ is all you need, until Christ is all you have," she said, then added, "Never be afraid to trust an unknown future to a known God."

[18] "So we fix our eyes not on what is seen, but on what is unseen, since what is seen is temporary, but what is unseen is eternal."
2 Corinthians 4:18 NIV

Accounts of men and women in service often reveal a divine touch that brought them the hope that they desperately needed. Verse 4 in Psalm 23 KJV, only six short verses long, tells us, "Yea, though I walk through the valley of the shadow of death, I will fear no evil, for thou art with me…" Can there be a shadow without a light on the other side?

We can look through books, quotes, and testimonies in every language of how people's lives have turned from despair, crime, addictions, bad marriages, destructive habits, even attempts to end their own lives, after a person decides to consider God and His promises.

Experiencing God, a study by Henry Blackaby and his son, emphasizes that "God is at work all around us all the time," and it's not that difficult to find Him because He is pure love.

Frances Jane Crosby found God despite her blindness that began when she was only six weeks old. As the story goes, at six weeks of age, Fanny seemed to have a minor eye infection. Her parents took her to a doctor who applied a hot, mustard-based ointment to Fanny's eyes, believing it would draw out the inflammation. Instead, the treatment left her completely blind. Four months later, her father died of pneumonia, leaving her mother a widow at the age of twenty-one. Believing that God would sustain them, Fanny's mother and grandmother, Eunice, began teaching Fanny about God's love. During her lifetime, Fanny Crosby was married, had one child (who died in her sleep soon after her birth), and is credited with writing *eight thousand* hymns. She lived to be 94 years old.

"It seemed intended by the blessed providence of God that I should be blind all my life, and I thank Him for the dispensation. If perfect earthly sight were offered me

tomorrow, I would not accept it. I might not have sung hymns to the praise of God if I had been distracted by the beautiful and interesting things about me."
Fanny Crosby (1820-1915)

"If there is only one strand of faith amongst all the corruption within us, God will take hold of that one strand," Oswald Chambers encouraged readers, in his book *Not Knowing Whither*.

The Bible tells us, "The people walking in darkness have seen a great light; on those living in the land of deep darkness a light has dawned." Isaiah 9:2 NIV These words were written by Isaiah in the 8th century BC. Jesus later declared, "I am the light of the world. Whoever follows me will never walk in darkness but will have the light of life." John 8:12 NIV

The prophet Isaiah wrote this of God, "It is He who sits above the 'circle' of earth…" (Isaiah 40:22 ESV) while much of mankind lived in fear of walking too far and falling off the edge!

You may be surprised to learn that Buddha also prophesied about Jesus in the 5th century BC. In the Buddhist scriptures, his followers are given a description of who Buddha believed would be "The Holy One," to come:

"The Holy One who will rescue the world in the near future will have scars on his hands and scars on his feet… In His side, there is a stab wound. His forehead is full of blemish and scars. The Holy Person will be like a golden vessel, a very large one, that will carry you across the cycle of suffering until you pass over to Heaven…you will have a new spirit that shines like a lightning bug come down from Heaven above and dwelling in your hearts. And you

will be given victory over all your enemies…and when you die, you will not come back to this world again."
(Steve Cioccolanti, From Buddha to Jesus)

Often parents are in the dark about how to raise their children or how to communicate with them once they are grown. Mary talks about being criticized for being so strict with her children; in other words, Mary didn't do everything for them. She wanted to teach them to do things themselves. "My mother taught us to learn to do things for ourselves," Mary says, "and that's not always easy." All of us have seen screaming children throwing fits because they know that their moms or dads will run to them with whatever they want, hoping to stop them from crying. Sometimes they grow up thinking the world owes them something. "That's not how my mother did it, and that's not how we did it. If we said it was time to go to bed, sometimes we would hear the crying for longer than we wanted to, but we didn't interfere by running into their room asking what they wanted. We waited outside their room and were relieved when they finally fell asleep. After they knew the routine, going to bed became easier for all of us."

In Henry Miller's short story, "Why the Butterfly Died," a guru held a cocoon in his hand, and naturally, a little boy wanted it. The guru gave it to the boy after the child promised *not* to help the butterfly when it was ready to emerge. The boy took the cocoon home, and when he noticed it moving on its own and saw the cocoon beginning to split slightly, he couldn't resist putting his fingers into the crack and helping the wet butterfly out of its encasement. The butterfly wasn't even strong enough to stand! Crying, the boy ran to the guru with the wet butterfly that wasn't moving at all. The guru knew that the boy had broken his promise and explained that the struggle inside the cocoon was what made the butterfly's wings strong enough to emerge and fly! Similarly, our human struggles can make us stronger, and eventually, we can see our way out of what once confined us.

Mary says she was a learn-to-do-it-yourself mom; that is, she taught them how to get what they needed, not necessarily what they wanted. "When Chris was only two years old, he started coming into our room in the middle of the night asking if he could have a bottle of water or milk. The first time, I showed him how to go to the kitchen, open the refrigerator, and get the bottle of water or milk that was waiting for him in the inside of the door. Then, I let him know how important it was for all of us to get our sleep. The second time, I showed him again, step-by-step, and told him that the next time, he should quietly try to get the drink himself. One night I heard him climbing out of his crib, heard the pitter-patter of his feet going to the kitchen, heard him open the refrigerator door... then I heard the whole scenario in reverse until he got back to his room and into his bed. Every time he got up, I heard him from the other room and waited for him to get back into his crib."

Teaching a child how to do basic things—get dressed, brush teeth, tie shoes, etc. builds self-esteem. Here's a short personal account of how Mary saw it building self-confidence:

The family went to Disney World when their sons were young. Walking down the famous Main Street U.S.A, they saw a lot of vendors with good things to eat. Gordon asked for a popsicle. Mary gave him two dollars and told him to go get a popsicle while she watched. Gordon came back with no popsicle, so Mary asked him for the two dollars back, and they walked until they saw another ice cream vendor. Again, Gordon asked for a popsicle. Mary gave him the two dollars, and the same thing happened. Gordon came back and gave her the money. At the third vendor, Gordon took the money and spoke to the vendor, "May I please have a popsicle?" Mary says that children who are raised with their parents doing everything for them and giving everything to them often don't realize that they may be building a co-dependent relationship with their children. "We wanted to raise our sons to become men who could think for themselves and who could stand on their own two feet. We also wanted to develop a relationship of trust with our sons."

In 2011, a Yale Law School professor named Amy Chua popularized the term "tiger mother" or "tiger mom" in her book *Battle Hymn of the Tiger Mother*. It was supposed to be a story of how Chinese parents are better at raising children than parents in other cultures, namely in western ones. The notion generated a series of TV programs in Singapore, mainland China, and Hong Kong. A "tiger mom" is defined as one who brings up her children in a strict, traditional Chinese way, stressing high academic achievement at a young age and working hard to accomplish excellence in every field. Some tiger moms go overboard with strict rules and expectations.

On the contrary are "elephant parents," who believe that it takes a whole village to raise their only child, and they depend not only on the community, but on parents, grandparents, aunts, and uncles to support them in parenting. Elephant parents try to keep things as flexible as possible and aren't big on discipline. I suspect an elephant parent wrote in a description that elephant parents "are nurturing...and refrain from raising their voices." There's often no set bedtime or dinner time.

Mary and Jim didn't have a whole village when they were raising their children in Miami. Jim was studying to become a doctor; Mary worked two and sometimes three jobs, and they had two young sons. They didn't have relatives, only colleagues, and the money was tight. Being Christians balanced everything in raising their children. The Bible says you love your child if you draw lines for discipline. In fact, the Bible says, "The Lord corrects the people he loves and disciplines those he calls his own" (Hebrews 12:6 CEV). Leave it to the world to come up with tiger parent, elephant parent, dolphin parent, helicopter parent! The Bible says the world will make up things to separate us from the reality that our Heavenly Father knows best. If a child is loved and taught self-worth, compassion for others, and a healthy reverence for a living, loving God, the rest of the world will reap the benefits.

Many communities who are being served by ChenMed are reaping the benefits of the direction, love, and compassion that Mary and Jim instilled in their sons. In fact, some of the most beautiful offices are being built in very low-income communities to serve as beacons of hope for the underserved. ChenMed makes it a point to hire local people in their new clinics and to partner with local agencies who are there to improve the communities.

Dr. Gordon Chen puts it so beautifully when he describes the mission of the Chen family: "Our Family purpose here at ChenMed is to glorify God by spreading more love and promoting better health in all who come into contact with ChenMed. We have this vision to be America's leading primary care provider transforming care of the neediest populations. As a Christian family who started the organization, we feel called to serve the neediest communities, not only because we've been needy ourselves, but because we feel that God has just empowered us and given us the opportunity to help those communities in the greatest need. You see, we've suffered as a family; we have fought through cancer; we've struggled through poverty, and now that God has saved us through those situations, through His mercy and grace, we feel this tremendous calling to spread this model of better healthcare to all the communities that could benefit, starting with the neediest communities, and that tends to be the communities right now that are poor, underserved, under resourced... and that's where we feel we are called."

"For the message of the cross
is foolishness to those
who are perishing,
but to us who are being saved
it is the power of God."

1 CORINTHIANS 1:18 NIV

Chapter 21

In 2003, the same year when Dr. Chen was given his misdiagnosis and prognosis of two to three months to live, his older son, Chris, and his wife, Stephanie, gave him an ultrasound image for Christmas. "His name is going to be James," they told him. Mary said when Jim saw the ultrasound of prenatal James, he was overcome. "I saw tears in Jim's eyes," Mary told me. "He told me later that when he saw the ultrasound image, he *knew* that he would recover from the cancer. And he did!" Dr. Chen went back to work full time in 2005. Today he is cancer-free.

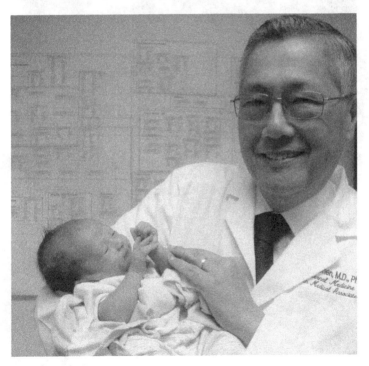

THE MIAMI HERALD, JUNE 25, 2006.

In July 2020, Dr. Chris Chen was taken out of ICU and began recovering from the death-dealing effects of COVID-19. He attributes much of his recovery to a six-foot-tall Jamaican woman named Helen, his ICU nurse, who Chris said may have been a former drill instructor. My guess is she is probably one of God's best! She often showed up in the middle of the night to order him to breathe, and they "reached an understanding." When she told Chris to do what had to be done, Chris did it. ("My Severe COVID-19: It felt like dying in solitary confinement," by Christopher Chen, August 28, 2020.) ChenMed anticipates administering 50,000 COVID-19 vaccines by Mother's Day 2021!

> *"Do you not know that your bodies are temples of the Holy Spirit, who is in you, whom you have received from God? You are not your own; you were bought at a price. Therefore honor God with your bodies."*
> **1 Corinthians 6:19-20 NIV**

Over the years, the pictures have said it all!

CHRISTMAS 2004 WITH FIRST GRANDCHILD.

The message inside the most recent Christmas card reads: "I bring you good news that will cause great joy for all the people." Luke 2:10 NIV

ChenMed continues to maintain excellent standards of care for their patients, specifically for the elderly who are underserved. While many medical facilities refuse Medicaid patients, ChenMed embraces them and treats them as VIPs.

An employee in a new clinic recently asked Mary why ChenMed builds such nice offices in communities that reflect poverty. "We want to impact the entire community for the better," says Mary. "We hire local people to provide jobs and we partner with other foundations that can help these communities improve their quality of life." Often when we visit the new clinics, an employee will greet us and thank us wholeheartedly for coming to their neighborhood. ChenMed wants employees, partners, and especially their senior patients to be treated with respect and dignity, to learn to stay healthy, and to enjoy their grandchildren and teach them healthy lifestyles, as well.

Outside the ChenMed offices, Chen volunteers partner with 40 local foundations to improve the quality of life in surrounding communities. The company has reached out to sponsor literacy programs, health education programs, food collection and distribution, transportation, housing, and basic needs (even laundry services!) for the neediest in the communities.

At this time, ChenMed stands as a privately-owned medical company that is expected to reach 100 primary care practices in twelve states by the end of 2021. The company is a provider of choice for Medicare Advantage insurance plans. In 2020, ChenMed was honored to be named as one of Fortune magazine's top 53 companies on its "Change the World" list for taking on some of society's most difficult problems among the neediest. Their company has grown to include Chen Senior Medical Center, Dedicated Senior Medical Center, and JenCare Senior Medical Center. Their clinics and influence continue to multiply. ChenMed has generously supported local as well as international efforts to enhance the lives of others through gifts and services.

The Chens gratefully acknowledge that God has blessed their family profoundly during their fifty years of marriage to be celebrated in August 2021. Their family-owned company employs six adult family members, each holding an important position at ChenMed, each contributing a unique talent, with everyone working together. The icing on the cake is eight of the best grandchildren ever to walk the face of the earth who affectionately call Mary 奶奶 (Nai nai = "Grandma").

[31] "But they that wait upon the LORD shall renew their strength; they shall mount up with wings as eagles; they shall run, and not be weary; and they shall walk, and not faint."

Isaiah 40:31 KJV

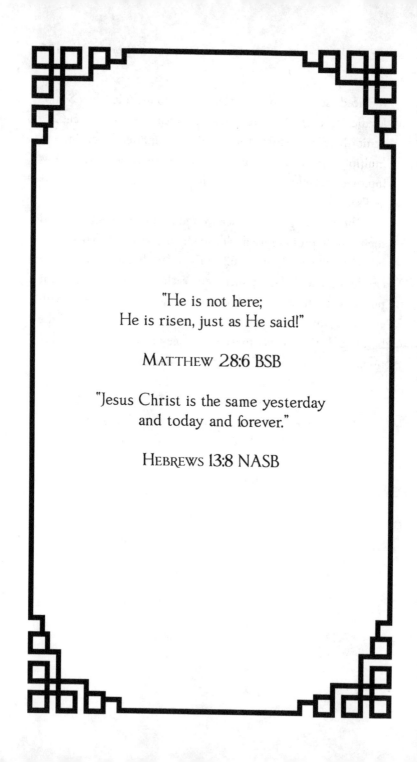

"He is not here;
He is risen, just as He said!"

MATTHEW 28:6 BSB

"Jesus Christ is the same yesterday
and today and forever."

HEBREWS 13:8 NASB

Acknowledgments

"Because he loves me," says the LORD, "I will rescue him; I will protect him, for he acknowledges my name."
Psalm 91:14 NIV

We thank God for His hand in writing this book. We thank Him for our friendship and gifts in making this happen.

In addition, we thank our families and friends who encouraged us and helped us along the way. Your love, support and encouragement are reflected on each page.

We would also like to thank ChenMed's Jeff Opperman, Vicky Durkin and Alina Maruri for their help and support. We gave you a raw manuscript. You gave us back a finished book.

We are forever indebted to the professionals at Morgan James Publishing. Your confidence in this story and belief that others might benefit from reading it was a gift. Your expertise putting the story into book form was a blessing.

Thanks too, to all the countless believers who boldly share the Gospel!

About the Authors

Mary Shao Mei Lee Chen is the co-founder of ChenMed. She serves as the organization's Chief Market Development Officer.

A woman of strong Christian faith, she created, along with her husband, Dr. Jen-Ling Chen, a mission-driven healthcare organization caring for the most fragile and underserved senior citizens in America. Her devotion and commitment to serving patients with VIP Care creates better health and superior quality of life for seniors across 12 states. Her leadership differentiates the ChenMed brand with its high patient satisfaction and net promoter scores in the low-to-mid 90s at each of the company's approximately 80 medical centers — a score unprecedented in the healthcare industry.

Mary Shao Mei Lee Chen's goal is to glorify God and spread his word. His willingness to give Mary Shao Mei Lee Chen and her family a purpose beyond what they ever asked for or imagined drove her to share her story with believers and non-believers alike.

Krissie Schuster Cilano and her husband have led 100+ American, European, and Asian Christian mission teams into Europe and Thailand over the past 21 years. She has witnessed lives changed for the better (including her own) after discovering how to experience and enjoy God's presence.

Knowing God better and making Him known is her passion. She loves to watch Him work when situations seem impossible and has been profoundly privileged to learn the truth of the Bible from gifted teachers as well as from personal experience. God has shown her things she would never have known if she hadn't stepped aside to focus on Him. He has shown her extraordinary favor and has become her purpose, freedom, joy, and sanity.

Krissie Schuster Cilano lives and breathes God stories, and The Chronicles of Nai nai 奶奶: Beyond What Was Asked for or Imagined! is one among His best!

Resources

ChenMed
www.chenmed.com

ChenMed Cares Foundation
home.chenmed.com/chenmed-cares/

Amos Health & Hope Ministries in Nicaragua
www.amoshealth.org

The Faith Foundry
www.faithfoundry.org

World Outreach Ministries
www.worldoutreach.org

**GuideStone Financial Resources
of the Southern Baptist Convention**
www.guidestone.org

A free ebook edition
is available with the
purchase of this book.

To claim your free ebook edition:

1. Visit MorganJamesBOGO.com
2. Sign your name CLEARLY in the space
3. Complete the form and submit a photo of the entire copyright page
4. You or your friend can download the ebook to your preferred device

Morgan James
BOGO™

A **FREE** ebook edition is available for you
or a friend with the purchase of this print book.

CLEARLY SIGN YOUR NAME ABOVE

Instructions to claim your free ebook edition:
1. Visit MorganJamesBOGO.com
2. Sign your name CLEARLY in the space above
3. Complete the form and submit a photo
   of this entire page
4. You or your friend can download the ebook
   to your preferred device

Print & Digital Together Forever.

Snap a photo   Free ebook   Read anywhere